libro
futbol
.com

AL GOL SE
LLEGA LEYENDO

A 21-YEAR EXPERIENCE IN ELITE FOOTBALL AT ATHLETIC CLUB BILBAO (1996-2017)

THE GAZE THROUGH PSYCHOLOGY

Translated by John O' Neill

María Ruiz de Oña

The Gaze Through Psychology/ Ruíz de Oña, María - 1a ed. -
LIBROFUTBOL.com, 2021.
210 pages; 15,2 x 22,9 cm.

ISBN 978-987-8370-44-6

1.Psychology. 2. Sports Psychology I. Title.
CDD 796.023

THE GAZE THROUGH PSYCHOLOGY
by María Ruíz de Oña

© 2021– LIBROFUTBOL.com

Cover design: Luciano Medvetkin
Layout: Luciano Medvetkin
Author's photo: © María Ruíz de Oña
Cover pictures: © Shutterstock

LIBROFUTBOL.com
Olga Cossettini 1112 - office 8F - City of Buenos Aires - Argentina
ediciones@librofutbol.com - whatsapp +54 9 11 2215 1982

1st edition: July 2021

ISBN 978-987-8370-44-6

INDEX

INTRODUCTION 5

Chapter 1
THE FRAMEWORK 13

Chapter 2
THE PSYCHOLOGIST 23

Chapter 3
THE PLAYER 35

Chapter 4
THE COACH 41

Chapter 5
COACH-TO-COACH LEARNING 75

Chapter 6
THE ORGANISATION 101

Chapter 7
LIGHTS AND SHADOWS DURING
THE LEARNING 109

Chapter 8
CLOSURE 141

Chapter 9
STARTING OVER 187

EPILOGUE 195

THE AUTHORS 201

BIBLIOGRAPHICAL REFERENCES. 205

FOOTBALL CATEGORIES
SPAIN & ATHLETIC CLUB BILBAO. 207

INTRODUCTION

After working for 21 years at Athletic Club Bilbao, I can now say that I have learned, changed and built up many aspects of myself both personally and professionally; I could list them all, but above all what has been changing is my way of looking at the world and specifically my professional world, *that being in Education of Player Development through Coach Development.*

It is normal that professional football is the benchmark for people working in the world of football; however, working on the development of people in any context involves broadening our horizons.

In Athletic Club Bilbao, I have had the possibility to build this other perspective of work, whose focus is to develop the potential of the player's person through the development of the coach's potential; in this case, to promote an active, thinking and conscious player, insofar as they participate in their own learning. It was Jack Mezirow[1] who expressed that learning was

---

1   American sociologist, founder of the theory of transformative learning.

"evolving towards learning with a critical transformative perspective", and one being based on the hermeneutic-comprehensive paradigm cited by Reale[2]. This is where hermeneutics is the art of interpretation or, phrased even more generally, the art of understanding and therefore directed towards the internal rather than external concepts that are signified only by the empirical universe, i.e. a holistic meaning in contrast to only units of measurement or a person's self-point of view only. As a leader this means not only using the knowledge gained to help others to evolve but more importantly use this knowledge to develop and evolve yourself first. In elite football, many times this requires that a change needs to happen within the coach first before expecting a change within the players.

This implied a change in the role of the football technicians, including the psychologists, for whom, in addition to psychological intervention, the world of knowledge generation was opened up to us; in this case, knowledge of the game and knowledge of the player in the game through the creation of optimal learning contexts; that is, education.

Several factors were needed for this change of focus, with the most important being to broaden *The Gaze* of the professionals who work with the player, from the football technicians to the educators.

---

2   Giovanni Reale, Italian philosopher.

In the words of Juan Domingo Farnós: *"This changed from the traditional teaching paradigm to a learning paradigm."*[3]

Two years after I left Athletic and with the perspective that time brings, I realise that almost all my work with coaches and players has been focused on educating their eyes. This is to gaze through understanding, to look in order to understand the world and to look at oneself in order to understand oneself in one's world. Learning to watch and gaze has been the core of my work.

When I speak of *The Gaze,* it is important to understand that this learning concept comes from a Spanish word known as La Mirada[4]. When translated from Spanish to English, this literally means *'The Look'*, but in the context of my work it means the 'gaze through psychology'. Its origins are often associated within the world of art and it is an experience that is lived in the first person, including seeing, feeling, listening, understanding, and intuiting. In essence, it means that the way we look at development should constantly be evolving and therefore our gaze is always alive and active, looking at what's in front of us and what is within us.

At Athletic Club Bilbao, this meant that even though the players may be 'quarried' from the same land of

---

3   Spanish researcher and specialist in education.
4   Marius Bomholt, Artworks that Look at You (and Themselves), Reflections on the Gaze (La Mirada).

the cantera[5], it is important to always find something new in the person in front of you and within oneself. So what happens to me when I gaze? This type of look does not seek anything concrete. It does not have a goal. Instead, the gaze is an attitude that embraces what is emerging and what is coming towards you. The gaze helps to integrate what is outside and what is within oneself. However, many times the thinking mind obstructs the gaze when it analyses, judges, evaluates and seeks objectives. The mind blinds the gaze when it lives it as something separate from what is happening inside of oneself.

The Gaze is also akin to seeing something new in a painting that has been hanging on the same wall for decades. More so, it is similar to how a self-portrait by an artist shows what they see and don't see about themselves. What self-portrait does a game of football paint for the players and the coaches? What are they hiding in these self-portraits? La Mirada is a guide that captures vulnerability from moment to moment, and by letting it lead the club and the teams it can promote learning. In his book *"Ways of Seeing"*[6], John Berger wrote how seeing comes before speech: *'the child looks and recognises before it can say any words'*. This is seeing that establishes our place in the surrounding world. We can explain that world with

5   Cantera, from the word 'quarry', the term is widely used in Spanish football to refer to youth academies.
6   John Berger, novelist and visionary writer who helped transform how art is looked at and perceived.

words, but we can never undo the fact that we are surrounded by it. The relation between want we see and what we know is never settled. Just as in the case of Athletic Club Bilbao, we were surrounded by our cantera, and through La Mirada we could never settle on what we saw and what we knew. As Berger concluded, *'There is an ever-present gap between words and seeing, and the way we see things is affected by what we know and what we believe'*.

In order to understand what we do, how we do it, and from where we do it, we need to open our horizons and open our gaze. Learning to watch, look and more importantly *gaze* is a necessity in every profession. Throughout this book and for the readers' understanding, *The Gaze (La Mirada)* will be interlinked with words that make up its core meaning. This includes previously stated and further words such as; gaze, looking, watching, listening, viewing, the eyes, the ears, the words we use, and understanding and working with the silence within a conversation.

Within *The Gaze*, I am not only referring to where we put the focus when we intervene in conversations, meetings, when we plan, when we train and compete, but to what we look at and from what inner place we look from. This specific gaze has to do with how I professionally and as person, am in the world. It entails understanding and openness, and it embraces what is in that moment, be it lights or shadows of oneself or of the reality that is in front of us. It welcomes what emerges and it involves being present in what I'm looking at and being available to it. The gaze understands looking at what is seen and what is not seen, but is felt or intuited. It requires looking beyond and seeing what others don't see and is a way of being in the world: present, available and creates critical questioning.

If someone were to ask me how I have evolved as a professional, I would say that what has made me grow the most has been the evolution of my gaze in breadth, in depth and in its inner game, in this case elite football.

For that to happen, I had to learn to gaze by understanding the following questions:

- **Where to gaze?** In everyday matters, in conversations, in what I heard on the training fields, in the games.
- **What's happening?** This is the question that guides the eyes. What's going on in the here and now?
- **How to gaze?** Being open to what is coming and to what is emerging; being available, leaving space for what is coming to gaze at and then looking for the questions that will help me to understand it.
- **Who's gazing?** Understand who's living this gaze. This means to understand what is mine and what is the other person's, my projections and their projec-

tions. It is also important to look at what part of one talks and what part of one hides when talking.

When you start working in a club where the focus is on talent development, you need to understand very well where that focus is, because otherwise we will not meet the real needs of either the player, coach or the organisation.

Over time, I realised that I needed to have my process of understanding, to be aware of this process and what it meant for me as a professional; among other things, to let go of many theories, beliefs and prejudices.

Someone once asked me: "Where are you looking from?" My reaction was to think what they meant. Going further, they expressed: "From what place inside you do you look and listen?" This interesting reflection threw me a conclusion: I look and gaze from my ideas and opinions, from my judgment and from my past.

This inner place from where I gaze was my great discovery: the inner part of me from which I am looking, listening or living. It forced me to work on removing veils, barriers and recognising what was mine, my beliefs, my fears, my prejudices and separating them from what the reality was showing me. This included looking at the players, the coaches, a philosophy, a history, the training sessions, the competitions and what the interaction of all this generated for me.

This question was my travel companion at that time and is still my travel companion today.

Going further into this type of graze, it looks at what's there, not what should be there or what I wish was there. It is nourished by the phenomenological, by what emerges in the here and now, and takes me beyond the justifying, theoretical or psychological explanations that may arise when I search for these answers. In such moments I try to push these explanations away and just let what I'm living through permeate me.

In this book I will try to show the evolution of the gaze through psychology, in this case mine through my experience at Athletic Club Bilbao over a 21-year period. I want to emphasise that this gaze is not an absolute truth or a reality from only my perspective. The words in this book are only part of an imprint of a person who passed through Athletic Club Bilbao, but that imprint is not only that someone nor is it ephemeral. Here, I will try to explain to you what this gaze meant to me in my evolution as a psychologist towards coach and player development in elite football. The aim being that this gaze can help you in your development.

CHAPTER 1

THE FRAMEWORK

At Athletic Club Bilbao, after the successes of the early Eighties, there was a sporting decline that was faced by changing the way of working in the Lezama Cantera (Athletic Club Bilbao Academy). From my point of view, this was the main competitive advantage of the Club. The organisation was facing a transformation in its culture, philosophy and working methods.

I remember the beginnings of this project being proposed in September, 1995 by José Mari Amorrortu, then coordinator of Lezama, with the implementation of a **Common Approach** for all our teams. Defining the path, sharing that vision and clarifying the sporting objectives were the first steps to be taken.

The strategic key to this transformation was to have a common approach. Behind it was that each football technician worked as a watertight department. The coach needed to understand that their team was tied to an organisation with long-term needs and that their players were in a training process for something bigger and much more complex than winning next Sunday. A broader, more global and more longitudinal vision was needed and primarily a holistic approach. At that time, the communication between the sporting coordinator and any coach was with a defined philosophy that was not about methodologies or planning, but about defining a path. Top-down coherence was a great challenge and this called for loyalty to the project.

The big objective was the evolution of the players with all decisions made with the player's progression in mind. This concluded that the value was the player, because it was believed that it was this outlook alone what made the Club competitive and allowed them to continue to compete at the highest level in football. The player had to stop being a means for the coach to win games; therefore, player development had to be an end in itself.

In this context, the first question arises: **What about the results?** Obviously, having results is fundamental, as it is a condition for the sporting and economic survival of the Club, but this does not make them the end of an organisation, at least in its stage of training players. Moving the case to an example, if a person doesn't eat, they will obviously die, but would we say that the purpose of a person is to eat?

We know that results are very important, but they are part of a process, or rather a consequence of it. Our actions produce those results. Normally, we put the focus and energy on that final part of the process, that being on the results, when the important thing needed is to take care of, improve and invest in the processes. Therefore, it is necessary to reflect on our actions and on the processes that actually lead to those results. This reflection is investigative, critical and causes another question to emerge: What drives me to act the way I do?

Seeing results as an end in themselves leads us to fall into a reductionist view of processes and people. Results are a very important indicator of organisations; they are a means, but they are not an end in themselves. The systemic view will say the only purpose of any organisation is its survival, and results are a very important means of achieving that survival. Still, the Lezama Cantera, as an organisation, was aware that they needed to deepen and broaden this understanding by placing the results in the player's development process.

All this defined the path of psychology in the Club and mine as a psychologist. The activity developed by the Psychology Department at Athletic Club Bilbao was oriented from and for the special philosophy of a club like Athletic, where the player is the value and the club are the learning process, the key point being to be able to be competitive. We worked on a training process where an active, thinking, and responsible player was encouraged to participate in their learning. That's why decisions and reflections were made around the needs of the player's development, that being where the player becomes the protagonist of their learning and development as a player. This implies a change of role in the coach who becomes a facilitator, a dynamiser of optimal learning in performance contexts, and who, in turn, functions as a teacher and as a learner. This is because the learning culture of the organisation is the engine and allows the people within this culture to be the required gears within that engine.

There has been three key elements in the blueprint of this exciting journey: listening, learning from and with the coaches, and questioning myself. All this within a learning culture in order to generate personal and professional development in the coaches; that is to say, that the coach integrates resources (working with objectives, managing dialogues, listening and making reflections through questions, giving and receiving feedback, etc.) through their own personal and professional development process.

Athletic Club Bilbao is a football club defined by its particular philosophy of competing only with Basque footballers whereby only players native to the Basque Country (Euskadi) are eligible to play for them.

The Basque Country is comprised of seven provinces and straddles the border between Spain and France, with Bilbao the largest city with an estimated 350,000 people. For more than a hundred years, the Bilbao entity decided to never count on players from outside the limits of the Basque Country. With this philosophy, and despite this self-imposed restriction, the club has never been relegated from Spain's top football league La Liga, a record held by only two other clubs: FC Barcelona and Real Madrid.

This particular way of tackling football is always under threat from the evolution of high-performance football. First it was the professionalisation, then the massive arrival of foreign players, and, in the last years, the Bosman Rule is the one that has changed the competitive context and, therefore, has conditioned the sporting performance of the Club. These situations have forced an improvement in the training work in a club that has the need of self-sufficiency, so it has had to face a change in its work as a football quarry (academy) that allows it to train a greater number of players capable of competing at the highest level. This change is the new strategic objective of the club, which will have to always create a new working style based on the training of players.

One of the defining characteristics of Athletic Club Bilbao is its respect for history. Fans and club keep their icons of the past alive by remembering with a special pride their achievements won by using a unique philosophy in world football. Having an identification with the Club is one of the keys to having an enthusiastic, faithful and constant passion for keeping these traditions alive. Now, the commitment is to modernise its working dynamics and to continue to grow to be at the level of the current football, and to continue doing so by maintaining that respect of history.

Athletic Club Bilbao, after the opening of the free market to European players and the growth of new clubs, could no longer compete either in structures or in recruitment. Therefore, improvement had to come through the understanding of this complexity and by awakening the potential with the maximum of stimuli for a better understanding of the game. That is why it was and still is fundamental to know for what and for whom we do our work. The old dilemma of means and ends was already present at that time in Athletic Club Bilbao. It was necessary to develop and go deeper into the preparation supports so that the players could give the best of themselves and, consequently, obtain satisfactory results. We wanted to create a model and style that would represent us.

The Psychology Department was making its debut in Athletic Club Bilbao in a full cultural transformation. It went from a more traditional philosophy focused on competition to a philosophy focused on the development of the player. Initially, the demand on the Department came from the way of reducing the competitive anxiety of the player, detected especially in the cadet category (players who were 14 and 15 years old). The intervention was done at three levels: players, coaches and parents. Over time, the intervention was extended to all the juvenile teams (players who were 16, 17 and 18 years old) and their coaches.

However, the key to these early years was to understand the reality that Lezama was experiencing in order to develop an intervention that would respond to the needs of this organisation. It was a priority to understand from the psychological intervention that it was not about preparing the player for Sunday's match but for something much bigger and further in time, i.e. preparing the player to be competitive in the professional world; preparing the player to be competitive in the first team. It was necessary to understand that the team was a resource for the development of the player and Sunday's match was not an end in itself but another resource for learning. All of this meant that a type of psychology had to be developed that responded to Lezama's needs.

During this time, the teams in Lezama won virtually every game with ease, and when the players reached ages where the competition was more balanced, the players did not embrace these difficulties. The players became conservative in their play and fear of failure surfaced, including signs of fragile confidence. On the contrary, the players regarded themselves highly, something that was not always expressed in the games. We saw that the results-focused approach led to players developing false self-esteem based on unrealistic results or external factors in the world of professional football.

The new project sought to identify the players, teams, coaches and managers by a way of dealing with situations, having values and a style, and without forgetting that you had to give up what you personally wanted to achieve. The search for an identity became our real focus that would give us our foundation.

One of the key measures taken was to implement a philosophy from the game based on the difficulty both in training (through drill exercises) and in competition. This is where the player played in the position that made them grow and by using open game systems where the objective was to expose rather than protect the player. With this, the aim was for the player to be able to face these stressful situations, at first naturally, until they became habits - for example, it would not be a drama for the player to stay in one-on-one situations, since it is a habit that has been resolved before and because it is part of their style of play - then the player assumes it normally.

All of this meant that coaches had to assume possible cons and risks, or even the possibility of losing. It meant greater self-demand and pressure from the organisation, which led to resistance to change and was intertwined with feelings of loss of power and status. These aspects were being fought as much as possible and divisions were appearing between the coaches who were following the project and those who disagreed for various reasons. The cohesion around the project would be a mission that would be left as a later objective.

CHAPTER 2

THE PSYCHOLOGIST.

BEGINNING AND EMPTYING (1995-2001)

My work as a sports psychologist at Athletic Club Bilbao began in 1995 through a collaboration agreement between Athletic Club and the University of Deusto, led by Jose María Amorrortu, director of the Lezama Cantera at the time. Some professionals who had studied at that University were offered the possibility of being part of that project. The project began with three psychologists.

The demand was focused on the players in the cadet categories (14-15 years old) because it was perceived that this was the age where competitive anxiety was beginning to be seen and players were abandoning their school studies over the years. It was a holistic approach, working with the players by offering them training programmes, meeting with their parents once a month and working on a day-to-day basis with the coaches. Over time, the work was extended to the juvenile teams (16-17 years old), and to the Third[7] and Second Division teams[8].

Four years later, the Club hired two psychologists and the Athletic Club Bilbao Psychology Department was established. Over time and for various reasons this Department ended up being formed by a single professional.

To begin, the first step was to integrate the figure of the psychologist into the daily life of Club's football academy. This meant dressing in the Club tracksuits but not getting involved in the football, not taking away the coach's authority and of course creating relationships of trust. As our work began, we did sessions with the players where we worked on concentration, confronting mistakes, negative thoughts, relaxation, and visualisation, all techniques typical of sports psychology that we had learned through our Master's studies and books. However, all that was left was these techniques and motivational concepts that sometimes felt like quick lifesaving pills. Something else was needed.

Those were the years of watching, learning and listening. It also involved the assignment of integrating

---

7   Third division team - known as Basconia, 18-year-old players (at youth age). They coincide in the team with 19-year-old players. They play the Third Division - Euskadi Group (fourth category of Spain senior league). They play against clubs with senior players.
8   Second Division team - Bilbao Athletic. They play in Second B or Second Spanish Division against senior professional teams.

psychology along with other areas, such as medical services, physical preparation and in the preparation and planning of sports tasks with the teams. The aim was to get coordinators and coaches to work on psychological aspects as well as physical, technical and tactical aspects and include them in their planning. This included providing time (inside and outside training) and resources (collaboration, involvement and commitment) to optimise the performance of the player and the team.

The psychological work was taking place in Lezama step-by-step by paying special attention to the rhythm that the coaches were taking in order to understand the psychology and the psychologists in their day-to-day work without it being a threat. Listening to them, accompanying them and being present in their environment were the keys to generating confidence in the coaches so that in the following stages we could work together in the training of the player. Even so, there was still a long way to go, and above all there was a need to build an intervention from the psychology of sport that was appropriate to the needs of this club.

In those years, the work with the player was more focused on emotional support than on learning. The player would come to unload their complaints about the coach or any other situation and the psychologist would listen, encourage and advise them. The player took a victim role and didn't move forward. On the other hand, the coach also took a passive stance by waiting for the player to heal. Thus, the psychologist had a role as a saviour and as a counsellor of the players and although there was information that was shared with the coach, the problem for the player was with the coach and for the coach the problem was with the player. In the end, we were building a way to work based on that it was the player who has a problem. Besides this, as the psychologist, I had normally already arrived at the diagnosis made by the coach - lack of confidence, fear, problems at home – then the psychologist had to solve it. However, this kind of solution application soon stopped working and I don't even know truthfully if it ever did work.

This brought me to my first question: **Am I prepared to work in a club whose focus is on the development of a person's potential**?

Most of us think or have thought at some point that we are ready to develop talent and train players; indeed, we think our approach is of great value. However, looking back in time, I think that starting from the premise "I am ready" is a wrong premise. And I do not judge whether we are ready or not, but the initial approach I now see must be another one, meaning it's not so much about being prepared to develop players but about being open to understanding the reality that lies ahead.

When we arrive at a new job, presenting ourselves as experts gives us security, but at the same time it can limit the development of the player and the rest of the people around you. I often work with coaches on this question: Why should what served you, what is now your experience, serve your players equally today?

I realised I was working from 'I know and I'll show you'. My proposal was defined more by my past learning than by knowing how to look at the future possibilities that may emerge in the player and the coaches (Otto Scharmer, 2009)[9]. This meant a radical change in me. I understood that I needed to look, to be open to what was appearing in the moment and to understand what was going to make me grow as a professional.

Javier García de Andoín[10] qualifies this growth as a professional in the dialogues we shared at the Self Institute at this time as: *"Talent development has no shortcuts; it is a long journey and above all through oneself. For talent development or high performance you have to go the difficult way if you want a real change. There are no shortcuts on this journey, no short or superficial trips and by that I mean motivational videos, slogans, quick fixes ..."*

---

9   A German professor at the MIT Management Sloan School in Massachusetts and the creator of Theory U, included in the book Theory U: Leading from the Future as it Emerges.
10   Philosopher, trainer and creator of the Self Institute.

Many coaches, professionals and psychologists look for recipes, buy technology, collect exercises, copy game systems from professional teams and stick to quick-fix solutions, but neither exercises nor video analysis alone develop talent. There is a big gap between developing people and this kind of action. The point is that this 'difficult' path involves learning and understanding from everyone that you meet on this journey.

Every day, I became more aware that these recipes and tools alone are not enough to solve this challenge of developing people. It was clear to me that if I expected any change in others or in the Lezama culture, then the change had to start with me.

I faced working on changing a philosophy by implementing a project based on the development of the player, understanding why the coach needed to learn and changing their leadership style and their approach to the player. The fulfilment of these premises implies the transformation of a club's culture. However, that was still a long way off, I didn't know how to do it, but I did know where to start: by questioning what I was doing and how I was doing it. All this was confronting me with myself and with what I had done so far.

I began to invest many more hours into my work as I needed to be there, to see and feel the different moments that a player and coach goes through: the training, the before and after training, when they arrive at the Club, the conversations between the coaches and the players in the corridors, the pre-training talks and the talks being used to prepare the games. Additionally, to understand what happens to the player and coach when they lose, when they win, what they are like and how they live through the travel periods on the bus to games, what happened when games turnaround against them and likewise in their favour. Above all, to learn from all those moments, i.e. what was there? What was missing? How was it done?

These observations confirmed the importance of the coach in all these moments and the consequences of their interventions, sometimes facilitating and sometimes not so much. The questions was now clear: How to enter the world of the coach and the contexts they generate? How to give more quality to those conversations? Were they conversations or were they monologues from the coach that the player listened to?

I saw the great involvement that coaches had in trying to develop players who were ready to be professionals, as well as people who were ready to live a life with maturity. In general, the coaches worked long hours, were under continuous evaluation, could not show weakness, had to know everything and achieve almost everything. Who was I to give them a talk about what motivation is or advice about something psychological or propose them to work on concentration sessions with the players? Who was I to change them with the studies that in psychology are created from the competitions of a successful coach or according to the questionnaires that the players answer about the ideal coach? This is the moment that we had begun. I was wearing a tracksuit, but I was not yet integrated; neither I nor psychology had yet taken place.

This conclusion confirmed to me that I had to change from theoretical references, which gave me speeches and above all a lot of security, to more practical references; that is, to listen to people. I collected what the coach told me and took it with me to investigate and understand it; sometimes I would return some questions, but the truth is I intervened very little; I left the advice, opinions, agreements and disagreements for another time.

It's important to communicate here that it is not that I did not listen before, but I was doing it through the tracksuit, the psychology books, the theories and what it should be, etc.

During this time, if I didn't know how or why I was facing something, or if I didn't know how to do it, I would approach it without having answers or using psychological techniques that would usually hide my not knowing and my vulnerability. So, I threw myself in the deep end by listening to the coaches informally, doing so without any meetings or talks but within the midst of the moment they wanted. I realised that the coaches needed to be heard and that, despite being surrounded by other coaches, many times they felt an inner loneliness.

I remember going to the office to look for ways to reach that intimacy, that solitude, and to look for some clue that could open up the possibility of continuing to talk. I rarely gave the coach a solution, mostly because I didn't have one, and that was good for me because we were both working from our vulnerability. Sometimes a question or insight would come to me that seemed to open up a space for reflection in the coach.

In time, I hardly sat in the office. The truth is I didn't have a specific place to work either. I wasn't worried, as at some point, when the organisation would understand the needs of psychology, then that specific space would arrive. I spent all my time around the training fields and in the changing rooms, in silence, watching the training sessions, the games, the day-to-day life of the coaches and players, but without any concrete intention; it was more like watching what happens.

It is true that it was not easy. Sometimes I went home with the feeling of not having done anything concrete. However, I have to say that I was lucky enough to meet coaches who were very concerned and dissatisfied with their task of training players and, above all, they were able to see the same in me. I will always be grateful to these coaches for giving me permission to enter their worlds.

What was clear to me was that the first one who had to make a move to apprehend that whole world was me. I let go of what gave me security, for example, showing my knowledge, in this case of psychology, and with my restlessness and nonconformity I began to work.

The foundations seemed to be in place to start walking and building a different way of looking at player development. It was necessary to live several stages intensely to reach this end. In parallel to my process of understanding reality, the implementation of a **Common Approach** for all our teams in the Lezama Cantera, proposed by Jose Mari Amorrortu, opened up to the coaches the need to understand what this common approach meant. More so, what it would demand of them, and above all the need to learn to live in a new and unknown working culture at that time. The coach needed to understand that their team was tied to an organisation with long-term needs and that their players were in a training process for something bigger and much more complex than winning next Sunday's game. All of this required more than just being a professional player or studying for a Master's degree in Psychology, Sports Science or Football.

The big objective was, and still is today, the evolution of the players. Our decisions are made with the players' progression in mind. How would you respond to this philosophy? For my part, it was clear that I needed to leave behind that starting point in which I defined myself as the sports psychologist who tries to mentally prepare the player to face the competition by training their motivation, concentration, etc. I was beginning to understand that in Athletic Club Bilbao the need was different. But how? What to do? Where to look?

One question that activated me was: Do I train techniques with a player or do I develop the potential of the player's person? At that time I was already clear that I wasn't going to go down the road of teaching psychological techniques, but I still had a few years left to figure out what and how to do this concept of developing players.

CHAPTER 3

THE PLAYER.

LEARNING TO WALK (2001-2004)

In the year 2001, a new direction entered Lezama. Athletic Club Bilbao is one of the few professional clubs where its members elect a new president every four years and this time there was a change. The elections resulted in a remodelling of the facilities, where two offices for the psychologists and a room for teamwork were set up. Quite the luxury for us psychologists.

The entry and exit of coordinators, football technicians and other professionals made Lezama a living reality, which was modelled through a longitudinal process over time. The new direction gave continuity to the ideas inherited about the formation of the player; however, as in any process, it is necessary to define what we are modifying, what is gradually consolidating and what we must continue to shape with our daily bond. In this period, those innovative ideas were taking shape, but the difficulty was not in understanding the new ideas but in avoiding the old ones. These old ideas penetrated to the last corner of the brain of those who had been educated in this way.

The work of the Psychology Department was still focused on the player, as that part, which was considered the gear of the engine within the Club, still needed to be fixed. The intervention was focused on the second and third team of the Club (Second B and Third Division of Spanish Football League respectively). Since we were two psychologists at the time, we each took a team. This time, I was part of the staff of the third team, Basconia (18-19 year old players) and also worked when necessary with the cadets (14-15 year old players) and juveniles (16-17 year old players). Sometimes this was for individual needs and other times it posed a work programme with specific themes.

However, these programmes were rarely attended by the coach. I was aware that there was a great fracture in that relationship, as if it were something separate. With time I understood that the player's reaction or behaviour is related to the coach's reaction or behaviour. It was clear that it was necessary to integrate the two and to make the coach see themselves as part of the player's performance. This process was interesting. At first, a coach told me: *"María, can you talk to this player? I think they have a problem, or their personality doesn't let them perform well"*. So I'd ask them, *"What part of you can influence the player?"* The coach was thinking about it.

Over time, the wording of the question changed from the coach. *"María, what can I do about this player who is having trouble coping?"* There was still more talk of the player than trying to fix it, although it's true that there was some change in the player's actions in finding solutions. Finally, one day another coach said to me: *"María, I need to change something in me, I can't reach this player."* Here we were already talking about another gaze, which, for example, has to do with what I need to learn as a coach to improve my relationship with the player.

The investment in understanding football and Lezama's working culture was paying off and the figure of the psychologist was already part of the cantera (academy) teams for the majority of both the coaches and the players. The main tasks for the psychologists were to attend all the training sessions and team games, to work with the coaches and the players, whom we monitored individually, and as a team. We were in daily contact with the coach, we commented on the day-to-day, the needs, and the problems that arose, and from there we responded to the needs of the player and the team.

I realised that my job was more about responding to the emergence than scheduling psychology meetings with players. It was a much more constructivist view, where learning is an active process and the players are the builders of knowledge and therefore responsible for learning. From what we were experiencing at that moment and from the needs of the day-to-day, the coach and I prepared conversations with the players, including talks or dynamics with the team, which had to do with different themes that arose in the day-to-day. These were all considered to be part of the development of the player and involved facing the competition, improving objectives, dealing with resistance to change and understanding the emotions that arose. My view of the player was changing from trying to give them solutions or techniques, to helping them look at themselves and get to know themselves better.

With the coaches, we would prepare the talks before and after the games or training sessions. When the coaches asked me, I would give them feedback on their performance. Above all, I think my job with the coach was to help them reflect, to realise about themselves and their reactions and whether or not these were beneficial to the player. This reflection basically opened the way to a new challenge that broke with old paradigms regarding the figure of the all-knowing coach who teaches as they were taught or who does the training they did when they were a player.

However, the key to these first years was to understand the reality that Lezama was experiencing in order to develop an intervention that would respond to the needs of this organisation. It was a priority to understand from the psychological intervention that it was not about preparing the player for Sunday's game but for something much bigger and further in time, i.e. preparing the player to be competitive in the professional world. It was necessary to understand that the team is a means for the development of the player and that each game was not an end in itself but another means of learning. All of this meant that the gestation of a psychology that would respond to the Lezama's cantera needs had to begin.

The focus on the emotional support was broadened to a more transformative perspective. It was necessary to transform and to grow towards a culture of learning.

CHAPTER 4

THE COACH.

A NEW STEP (2004-2007)

In September, 2004, a new assessment of the situation of football at world level was made and the dynamic of our work that had begun in 1995, that was already very much evolved with respect to what we had previously started in Athletic Club Bilbao, was taken up again. Now the main concern of the Club's management was the training of the coach in this work philosophy and the top-down cohesion that would be required around it.

If we say that the player is our value, then the coach will be the most important piece in this process. The coach who came to work at the Lezama cantera had to understand a work philosophy and adapt to a methodology and a style of play that could not be done through an explanation or a talk. The new coordination was much stronger and clearer about working with the coaches. While also understanding the need to train the coach in a different philosophy and methodology; therefore on both sides, management and the coach were to be the key steps.

The first and most difficult step was to manage the resistance to change in many parts of the organisation. This change, when working with new methods, makes it difficult for coaches to retrain themselves and to interiorise a new style of leadership and a new role. In the players they are always new and different demands arising, in the leaders there is the difficulty of understanding a change, and in the media, criticism is always present as a reflection of their incomprehension, besides having to face the difficulty of changing the dialogue.

This reflection mainly opened the way to a new challenge that broke with past paradigms regarding the figure of the coach who knows everything, who teaches how they were taught or who does the training they did when they were a player. It was becoming increasingly evident that the coach entering the Lezama cantera needed training to understand this philosophy and how to translate it into their daily life.

In any cultural transformation, the key is to bring about a change in the way of thinking and feeling, not just in doing, which often comes about through obedience rather than conviction. This step was one of the tasks of the Department of Psychology: to materialise the philosophy and new values into actions and new meanings.

Openness to change and continuous improvement were two of the necessary values that we worked on to develop and implement the required foundations. This was done both in the physical space and by taking advantage of the conversations that arose in the training fields on a daily basis.

This new organisational culture had to be translated into concrete actions. That is why in the Department of Psychology we focused on rooting in certain foundations into people's daily lives with a form of work that was being implicitly built. Over time, these foundations became increasingly explicit and ended up being part of the process of implementing a learning culture.

FIRST FOUNDATION: PHILOSOPHY AND SPEAKING IN THE FIRST PERSON

The first challenge of the Psychology Department, which was already composed of only one person, **was to create a physical space**, a room with a round table and some chairs, where the coaches could sit and share their day-to-day experiences, fears and concerns. This project demanded a common way of working under the same travel plan for everyone, with very different paradigms from all those we brought with us on this journey. This space was more important than I thought at first. It was going to be the beginning of a big change in us and in our way of looking at player development. This physical space in the beginning acquired a confidence value and became a learning space. It was about all of us recognising the need to learn and what that involved: change.

In this way, the need for training and learning began to be seen in the coach. When a coach enters Lezama, they need to understand a working philosophy, with values already well established, so they have to adapt to a common methodology. In doing so, the coach will go through a small inner battle of feeling this loss of being the centre, of not having total power and will involve losing autonomy; that is, the organisation is no longer at their service, but they put themselves at the service of the organisation's needs. The coach, then has to be accompanied during this process.

This work philosophy was gaining strength and content. We talked a lot about what it was like to develop players and the differences in other ways of working. It was a guide on the road that helped to find us when someone got lost, didn't understand something or when egos, short-termism and authoritarianism with results appeared.

Over time, in 2007 or so, we collected all these reflections and presented them in a chart, which served as a reference for the new coaches who came to work on the project.

TRAINING AND COMPETITION FUNDAMENTALS

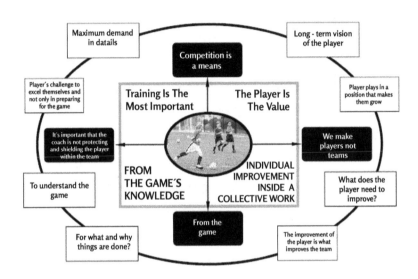

Edorta Murua, María Ruiz de Oña, Vicente Gómez

Group meetings were held, where the aim was first to understand, then to interiorise and finally, how to put this philosophy into practice. These meetings were very fruitful for the Psychology Department, as we all learned from each other and, for the first time, shared the pressures, fears and experiences of being a coach in Lezama. Very useful phrases appeared such as: *"When you enter Lezama, you realise that you don't know at least what you* thought", "admitting that you don't know is difficult and more so in football" or "in football you are valued for the results".

Some of the coaches came with the idea and conclusion of upgrading and promoting themselves. They had fear of losing and not fulfilling expectations. Other coaches instead came to see the training sessions of those who took more time to develop this necessary process. They stayed behind talking about their doubts, asking questions and learned to express their worries about understanding Lezama's reality.

A key step in this period was to integrate the concept of speaking in first person: "It happens to me that …", "I …", "I am in a moment that …", because this was the exact material we needed to work with; not with the common complaints, excuses or ideals, which do not lead to transforming anything.

This first person approach shared in our meetings was the door to the coach's work of self-knowledge. Over time, it became strange for us all to hear someone say, "It's the players that don't want compromises." Our reflection went in a different direction that stirred many interesting response questions: "And you, what are you committing yourself to? What's your difficulty there? What does that say about you?"

This way of working began to make a team and between all of us we were building a common approach in the psychological training with the player through conversations whose purpose was the professional development of coaches through self-knowledge.

We based our work on giving structure to the learning context, where the player focused on their improvements rather than on winning Sunday's game or being a starter. This was clear to us, but how did we convey it to the player?

SECOND FOUNDATION: LANGUAGE

"Language creates realities. When we speak, we intervene in the creation of the future, we shape our identity and the world in which we live. The way we speak is perhaps the most important factor in defining how we will be seen by others and by ourselves."

Humberto Maturana[11]

What do we talk about in our organisation? What do we talk about with our players? What reality do we want to create? If we wanted a player development culture we had to talk about improving, learning, goals, challenges and difficulties.

Our line of work is based on observing the coach's communication on the pitch and in the dressing room, and on giving importance to what we say and how we say it. Conversations with players, explanations of exercises, talks at the games, instructions and

---

11   A Chilean biologist specialised in knowledge and organisations.

corrections were the subjects of this work used with the coaches. This was done through recorded documentation, video recordings and awareness of the importance and consistency between what I say and what I do.

Maturana maintains that language is not innocent, but reflects the mental scheme from which we act. Analysing our language and the way we communicate was also another way of self-knowledge that helped us to become aware of our prevailing beliefs, while also giving way to beliefs that were more in line with the Club's philosophy of work through training and self-knowledge processes. We had to elaborate ideas, concepts and new languages that would help these processes transit and spread them to the coaches. This would allow their mental barriers, which were dependent on understanding reality from past schemes, to be lowered.

At this stage of change, it was not only a transformation of methods, profiles or structures but, in my opinion, it was a transformation of concepts, that all had meanings. What is a competitive player? What is winning? What is competition? What is success? What is effort? The basis of this process was to reflect on these concepts and come to unify their meanings. Consequently, we rethought the meaning of being a coach in Lezama.

We needed to create new discourses so that the players would think about concepts such as improvement, learning, overcoming and objectives. We were aware that many of the discourses heard in football were not consistent with our way of viewing development. Thus, for example, for us, whenever the player does not reach their maximum performance, even if they surpasses the contrary or are the best player on their team, we cannot say that we have won, that we have competed or that we have achieved the desired success.

The world of football is full of paradigms and beliefs, i.e. "football is like that", "results are king", "I train for the game". We could argue whether these are true or false, but that is not the question. It is about reviewing what are the psychological models, the beliefs that guide us as a club and if they really help us to get what we want.

The success of the transformation is when these concepts are internalised and this is the first step in my work with the coaches who are the main agents of change.

THIRD FOUNDATION: LEARNING TO LEARN & WORKING WITH OBJECTIVES

We understood the objectives as a means for the player to be able to focus attention on what will make them grow or solve the problems that the game poses to them. Above all, we wanted the player to be a tool to reflect on oneself, to look at oneself and to know oneself.

There is no point in training if I don't know what the objective is, if I don't see meaning in what I do (what for and why), and if I don't receive feedback on my performance. Learning is action plus reflection and through working on objectives we can achieve both tasks.

This dynamic was also used by the coaches, most of the time on their own initiative and other times because the objectives became part of the culture, and we all spoke from there platform. So not only did all the players have objectives, the coaches did too.

At first we had them written down in the changing rooms, the players were evaluated on the sheets, but the important thing was not so much the evaluation but that moment when the player reflected on what they had trained and how they had done it.

In addition, it helped the coaches focus their instructions and their corrections according to the player's objectives. It was a task that united the coach and the player in the challenge of improvement, and which opened possibilities of dialogue between them. Not only did the communication between coach and player increase in quantity and quality, but it also increased the deeper knowledge of the player. It helped to improve something that coaches often ask themselves: How to reach the player?

Over time, the objectives were managed by the coaches themselves, there was no longer a need to have them on the wall in the changing rooms. The players had internalised the objectives as part of their learning process thanks to the commitment of the coaches and the continuity given to them. From the youngest players (10 years old) of Lezama through to the third team (Basconia, 18-19 years old) of Athletic Club Bilbao, all worked with this system.

At this stage, I remember Txema Noriega, Lezama's coordinator during this period, told me: "You have to bring psychology to all of the Lezama cantera, not only to the players but also to the coaches," How? I thought and I told him at first that I couldn't, that individually I could do something with some of the coaches, but in a group it was impossible, that they didn't want to learn or work together. When I walked out the door, I took a breath and started to think about how to do it, again without knowing how or where. There was nothing left to learn and it is true that something more holistic was needed, something global that would embrace the whole process of the player's formation in an integral way.

The work of the previous years had been with a coach and a team. Now they were trying to break this coach-team pairing and move to a group of coaches who have the common goal of developing players.

> *"This led to another evolution in learning, where the reflection of practices took up more and more space and content. It remained to be discovered how the levers of change of that transformation would come to be." Andrea Ruffinelli[12].*

I was becoming more and more aware that my gaze was changing and consequently my role. I realised that in my day-to-day life I was someone who created and facilitated learning spaces with both players and coaches rather than deploying psychological health programmes for athletes.

I was lucky that a group of new coaches was starting in Lezama and that my work to immerse myself in the world of coaching was beginning to bear fruit. The older coaches came regularly to talk to me, I no longer needed to be on the field all day, and this was a great example for the new ones, who saw it as normal to work with the psychologist.

---

12   Andrea Ruffinelli, a Chilean expert in education, who expressed this reflection idea in 2007.

So the first thing I did was find a round table to sit at. It's funny because nowadays I don't even need a table. An empty room with some chairs is enough for me to create a learning space. This space was intended for the coaches to sit down and start reflecting in order to generate new knowledge about what we were doing and about ourselves.

At this stage of change, and as previously stated in the second foundation (language), it was not just a transformation of methods, profiles or structures but a transformation of concepts and meanings - What is a competitive player? What is winning? What is competition? - while the basis of this process was to reflect on these concepts and to unify their meanings of what it meant to be a coach at Lezama. Now I can say, 21 years later, I recognise that that resistance and that denial was the seed of the professional I am today.

But going back to that moment in Lezama, the first question we asked ourselves at that table was: What kind of player do we want to develop? And the second was a consequence of the first: What does this imply for our role as a coach in our day-to-day life?

In one of those meetings I wrote down something that Edorta Murua, the current director of football at the Aspire Academy in Qatar but at the time one of the most experienced head coaches at Athletic Club Bilbao, said:

"The reality of football tells us that players must be prepared to face the situations that the game will present to them. A game that demands rhythm, intensity, speed, determination, but also control, balance, pauses; in short, an understanding of the game. To understand the game you need to think about the game. We need players who think, who are autonomous, who understand the game and who make decisions for themselves."

This made me think that there was another step to take: to end the separation between those who think (coaches) and those who obey and execute (players).[13]And that, as we'll see later, meant rethinking the coach's leadership style.

I remember that, at first, it was I who took the initiative to bring us together. We divided the coaches into two groups, from the coaches working with youngest to cadets (10-15 years old) in one group and coaches working with the juvenile and third division teams (16-19 years old) in the other. We met every fortnight, and in between the meetings I met individually with each coach. The coordinator and the person responsible for the football methodology also participated in these meetings, proposing topics to be worked on, and I prepared the dynamics and facilitated the meeting.

---

13   Maite Dárceles, a consultant from Hobest, Gipuzkoa, with great experience in organisations.

We needed to create new discourses so that the players would think about aspects of improvement, learning, overcoming, objectives, all far from the mentioned clichés and beliefs typical of the world of football. I never intend to go in and see if these clichés are true or false, because I don't think that's the point, but it does alert me that we often take these clichés on and then that's it. At that time, it was a matter of reviewing what are the psychological models, the beliefs that guide us as a club and if they help us to get what we want.

It was difficult for me to lead this kind of meeting. If I really wanted these meetings to be spaces for transformative dialogue, my role had to go a step further. Today, it is something I continue to prepare for, because facilitating collective learning spaces implies a lot of preparation on the part of the facilitator; however, my focus now is not only on organising and energising the meeting, but on making the people who participate in it less and less dependent on me.

> *"It may be useful to have a moderator to keep the meeting going … But for it to work, it shouldn't be carried out like a job, although this occupation takes time. During this time, everything we have mentioned will appear and people will learn to be*

less and less dependent on the figure of the mode-
rator."

David Bohm[14]

The success of the transformation was that these concepts (success, winning, developing talent, learning) were being internalised by both players and coaches since they were the main agents of change. Little by little we began to share our experiences, fears and concerns. The conversations that arose in the meetings also evolved from technical and superficial aspects to experiential and profound themes. It was about recognising their need to learn.

Eventually it was the coaches who took the initiative to come and talk to me and who asked to continue their learning and deepening what we were doing. In this way, the need for learning began to be seen in the coach.

The conversation, the dialogue proposed by David Bohm[15] and the building of transformative relationships were to be the pillars of our psychological training. I realised that after six years I could say that psychology and I were integrated in the formation process of Lezama.

We were making progress and different questions were appearing: For what and for whom do trainee

---

14   David Bohm, American physicist with significant contributions to neuropsychology.
15   David Bohm, in his book 'On Dialogue' 1997.

coaches work? What do we talk about in our organisation? The coaches were joining together in this
critical work in order to create a culture of player
development.

We were building on the need to learn from coaches and players, doing so by working from objectives and on structuring training sessions so that there were spaces for reflection and dialogue with the
players. That is, we went from monologues and long
talks by the coaches to having the player participate
in them. From there, thought reflection led the talk or
conversation, while allowing us to exam our communication. This was another big step if we wanted to
transform the coach/player relationship.

In Lezama, we needed to evolve from a player who
obeys to a player who thinks. Learning became a value for us. It was about getting the player actively
involved in their own learning; therefore, it was not
about the coach coming in and telling you what to do.

"Knowing that teaching is not transferring knowledge, but creating possibilities for your own production or construction."

Paolo Freire[16]

The coaches at that time proposed to work with objectives. To this end, we reflected on why and what we were going to use them for, what meaning we were going to give them and how we were going to develop them. It was decided to see the objectives as a means for the player to be able to focus their attention on what will make them grow or solve the problems that the game poses, i.e. adversities, tactical problems, handling of emotions. The objectives should be a tool to reflect on oneself and to know oneself.

The usefulness of a training session was to have an objective and to know it, to know why and for what purpose I train something and to receive the feedback of my performance. "If the players have objectives, we should have objectives too," said a coach one day. Therefore, each coach set their goals and, above all, designed how they would set, track and evaluate them.

---

16   Brazilian pedagogue, who with his model of dialogue created a new path of relationship between teachers and students. Pedagogy of the Oppressed (1970).

Targets became part of the player's culture and became another doorway to open coach-player dialogues that were away from the typical morality of playing badly. They were focused on the needs, on the improvements of the player and this was something that coach and player had agreed beforehand. The relationship and the approach to the player was changing. The objectives, more than a motivating technique became a type of relationship that encouraged learning and awareness about oneself, about where I am and where I need to be in order to grow as a player and as a coach.

This work of the objectives as an awareness and self-knowledge began to give its results when you heard how the player talked about themselves, especially when they prepared the training sessions, pre and post-game talks, or when they talked with the coaches. For example:

"I've had this objective since last year and I think I've improved a lot since then. How many touches do I give in each action? I have to assess whether there's anyone better placed to receive the ball than me. Attacking and appearing in space at the right time, sometimes I am in the right space in the right moment, but I don't appear," said one infantil player (12-13 years old).

Speaking of amplitude: *"Attack space from position; amplitude control; not just fixate on the ball.*

And in the depth: I must move through the position, orient myself to see more things," said another cadet player (15 years old).

The objectives meant being a mirror that reflected how the players were internalising the common language, how much they were aware of themselves, what blind spots they had and, of course, the coach's work in all this was reflected.

When the coaches started working on their own objectives, it was a great initiative, which helped to make the learning process more natural for the coach. They asked each other for feedback to find out what their most important improvement objectives were, to be aware of their strengths and to update them. It was a big step and the initiative was in the hands of oneself.

At first, we wrote down the player's objectives on a sheet of paper, laminated it and hung it on the clothes hanger that each player had in the dressing room. The player then evaluated them on the sheets they had previously drawn up with the coach, and saw it as being natural to reflect on what they had trained and how they had done it.

In addition, and as already expressed, this dynamic of working with objectives was changing the way coaches looked at the player. We already know that not only did the communication between coach and player increase in quantity and quality, but it also helped to bring some conclusions to that very important question that that coaches often asked themselves: How do I get to the player?

While the objectives were managed by the coaches themselves and that there was no longer a need to have them on the wall in the changing rooms, it was clear to us that targets are useless if they stay on the wall. They have to be seen in action and they have to be moved to the field. We needed to create learning contexts; that is, to reinvent spaces in and out of training fields and likewise for games.

There was no end to it and the difficulties grew in the development of the player. Perhaps one of the most difficult tasks for coaches is to help the player grow. We saw that the focus of talent development was no longer just about scoring goals. We wanted the player to think, to decide, to communicate, to function as a team, to understand the game. So we had to ask ourselves: Are we creating spaces to be able to develop all of this? How are we creating them? This led us to conclude that such spaces can never have an end, that today's professional learning spaces have to allow more things to come to the surface.

LEARNING STRUCTURE FOR TRAINING SESSION

WHY AND WHAT FOR? WHAT ARE WE LOOKING FOR? WHAT DO WE WANT?	· Objectives of football exercise. · Transfer the objectives to real-life game situations. · What tools do you need to achieve these objectives?
THE RULES OF THE EXERCISE CAN'T DISTRACT YOU FROM THE OBJECTIVES	· The planning exercise sheets are hanging in the changing rooms and the players study them. ·To clear up any doubts. ·To focus player on the task.
THE PLAYER AND THE LEARNING	· Difficulties that I can find within the exercise. ·To remember that INDIVIDUAL OBJECTIVES are also in relation with the exercise objectives.

FOURTH FOUNDATION: CREATING A LEARNING CULTURE

During our daily conversations, the concern arose about how to bring the objectives into the trainings, the games and, above all, how to integrate them into the day-to-day of the Lezama cantera. To do this, we started with a structure that would allow for the learning to take place during training sessions and games. These moments were divided into before, during and after, and in each space we asked ourselves what we wanted the player to learn. From this, what we wanted and what the player needed to learn in those moments was appearing to us and more so how to approach them.

For example, what does a player learn before a training session or game? That's how we created the preliminaries. Before training, the session was left hanging in the dressing room so that the players could take responsibility for viewing it and then preparing it for training. They were the ones who explained the football exercises, the meaning of these exercises (why and what for), the objectives and the difficulties that could arise and how to overcome them and, above all, relate it to the objectives of each other. From this routine, came what the coaches called the "preliminaries". This preliminary moment of the training had already taken on its own identity as a learning space. In time, little by little, the other spaces took over. When I was talking to the coaches they would say: "We are better at using the period of closure (after training sessions or games)" or "we had a very interesting preliminary yesterday."

Together, we structured the before, during and after training sessions and games as learning spaces. For example, that is, we understood that before, during and after a game learning spaces are generated where the coach-player interaction gave form and content to that moment of learning.

ONE TO ONE ON THE PITCH

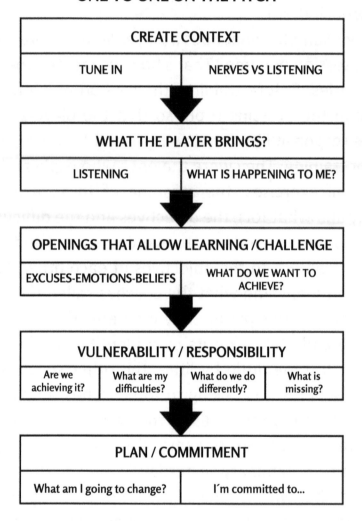

What does a player learn before training? The answer depends on the reality that we coaches believe. If the coach gives long explanations of tactics, the player will learn to listen or even obey the instructions, and we were clear that we wanted to get away from that type of learning. What we were looking for was to create interaction with the player so that they would learn to prepare for training with reflections like: What is the purpose of this football exercise? What does this exercise ask of me? What does the player learn before a game?

Many times, messages are given that are empty of content and very general. Other times, coaches pull out clichés like "let's have fun", "it's a game to learn"; however, at half-time those initial messages are not followed up, they are not reviewed or looked at to understand them more, and the messages will depend more on how the result is going than on the player's needs to grow.

GAME LEARNING STRUCTURE

That's why we decided with the coaches before the games to talk about what we had trained for during the week, what the objectives of the football exercises were in training, what we were looking for within them, what difficulties we were facing within them and how to overcome them. In addition, the objectives of each player were discussed and how they related to the objectives of the exercises. During the halftime breaks, the players discussed about whether or not they had achieved their objectives, what they were missing and what they were achieving. Little by little, the player was taking more prominence in these spaces, which helped with reflection and learning.

The language the players used was an indicator that the learning culture was increasingly pervasive in Lezama. More so, it's not a question of saying "I'm going to leave them alone today", as some coaches once told me, because the big difference is that in this case it would not be framed in a learning context and, in our case, it was part of a learning culture.

It was a very interesting experience to witness collaterally emerging leadership behaviours among the players. I remember one day being at a game and a coach from the academy came running into Lezama. They had a personal problem and they ended up arriving late. Just as they were about to enter the dressing room a delegate said, "Don't worry, they've already started preparing for the match." When the coach entered the room, the players were talking. One was on the board, one was talking and everyone else was listening. Someone took the lead and said to the others: "Let's start the talk." We are used to hearing phrases like "the kids don't want to commit" or "there are no leaders in the locker room", but did we let them lead? The moment we gave them an adequate space these leadership actions emerged; it was not by chance.

It was also very important for us to close off a training session or a game. What was the player taking home? It comes to my mind one Monday, when I arrived in Lezama and encountered four young players (10 years old) who were going to do their homework:

— *"How was Saturday's game?"* I asked them.

— *"Bad,"* answered one.

— *"Oh, yeah, why?"* I asked innocently.

— *"Because we lost,"* answered another, as if to say this one (me) does not know that if you lose it is logical that you have played badly.

— *"How did you play?"* I asked one.

— *"Good,"* he said.

— *"What about you?"* I asked the second

— *"Good,"* he agreed, and so did the third one.

— *"So who played badly?"* I questioned them.

— *"The team,"* this group replied emphatically.

At first I laughed, but when I walked into my office I felt that something wasn't right. What had these players learned from the game? What had they taken for themselves? It was clear that we had a lot of work ahead of us.

Understanding the role of the coach as a trainer became very interesting work towards making a reflection on how a professional coach prepares a game. A further comparison was reflecting on how a coach who didn't have a philosophy of developing players compared to a coach who has understood their role as a trainer prepares it.

How to face an important game with the training, drill exercises, planning and messages (i.e. the words we use) from the perspective of two different professional coaches who have two different approaches to development; (1) quantitative coach who is more focused on results and (2) qualitative coach who is more focused on being an educator.

SITUATIONS	PROFESSIONAL QUANTITATIVE COACH (RESULTS FOCUS)	PROFESSIONAL QUALITATIVE COACH (EDUCATOR)
Game planning - Objectives	- More focused on results than process. - More short-term vision than long-term vision. Players don't receive too many development objectives. Only the end results that matter.	- The coach remembers what and why do they do the specific football drills during the week. - Long-term vision.
TRAINING SESSIONS - Drill exercises - Messages to the players	- Drill exercises to prepare for the game. - Prepare the team to be strong for the game. - Build a team.	- Objective of the drills is to help players improve. - Planning focused on the needs of the players instead of focused on the opponent or game. - Build thinking players. Don't just give solutions. It's very important to use enquiry questions.
GAME - How do they prepare for the game? - messages	- All details controlled by the coach. - Coach prepares for the game and the players to cope with the game. - Messages focused on the team.	- Individual messages and feedback for each player. - Focus player on their needs to improve. - Don't protect the player or neither the team in their development that allows them to hide. - Expose the player to cope with their difficulties and blind spots.
BEHAVIOURS OF THE COACH - Before-during-after game - Managing the score	- Behaviours, reactions and communication are depending on the score and the performance. - Directions and messages in games are not coherent with the work that was executed in training during the week. - Coach pushes the player.	- More focused on creating a learning environment. - It's important to create the player's participation. - Game is a means and learning resource for the player. - Messages and words have a context, meaning there is coherence between the training sessions and the games.

COACHES

The last step was to allow the players to manage themselves before the games, and the coach had a facilitating role in all these dynamics. The players organised themselves as a team group or into smaller groups and talked about the week, objectives, difficulties and resources. This was part of a learning process and it was done in every game and tournament because now the player had acquired the resources to do it. We were evolving from a coach monologue to a dialogue between and with the players.

This change of gaze of how to face these spaces before or after the games and trainings led us to live these dialogues, questions and reflections. Doing so by the players and the coaches making these important learning moments very enriching. We were removing layers to get to the origin, to the essence and to understand what each one was doing.

Over the years, I was able to see the result of this way of learning through interaction and questioning before, during and after the trainings and games. All the coaches worked with this idea of generating first-person learning in the player and with the concept of developing critical thinking. They were coaches who had more or less experience in it, but the important thing is that they all tried. However, what began to happen is that the youngest players (10-11 years old) were more involved, but had less quality in terms of reflection and questioning. Everyone raised their hand to speak, as in school, but we taught them to listen to each other and respect each other's space for participation without the need to raise their hand. With the infantil category players (12-13 years old) it was a pleasure to share conversations as they had already internalised the habit of participating, preparing to train, reflecting after training and they still had not reached that moment of adolescence that seems to have forgotten everything, as in the cadet category players (14-15 years old). The juvenile category players (16-17 years old) had less participation, but higher quality. The player answered the coach's questions in depth, using the common language of Lezama's methodology, and in turn asked questions or gave opinions about the game or what they were facing at the time.

I used to participate in these dialogues in the background. I listened to the process of the dialogue, the content of what was being discussed and saw how the players were improving their ability to reflect in first person. Excuses, such as using 'us', which is no one, to evade responsibility and commitment, were disappearing. The coaches would ask me to be in the changing room with them to give them feedback on their questions, for example, or on the handling of the silences. On other occasions, some topics about emotions would come up and they would ask me to help them to energise it or even to intervene.

During the middle or at the end of the season, we would ask the players to explain a football exercise drill. I didn't really know what I was going to find, but I realised that the language that the player used was a reflection of the language the coach used. The common approach was beginning to bear fruit.

Over time, I was able to compare explanations from before the creating of a learning culture with explanations from after. I have saved some of the players' answers, like these:

"Three players attack and two defend. The attackers have to finish the play in goal. Attackers are superior to defenders who just have to cut off the play". This was the response of a player when their coaches related to them in a different way with the training explanations.

Another player from a group whose coaches were part of the construction of these learning spaces said: "In this exercise it is important to move the ball quickly and not drive on too much, because there is little room, and otherwise you end up crashing. It is also important to have mobility to find free spaces. In my case at least, it is important to orient yourself well. This exercise seems very effective because I am learning to orient myself better although I still have to improve. In defence, it is important to distribute the zones well and for that you have to communicate.

The bottom line is that with this exercise I am learning quite a bit."

The first player talked about the rules of the exercise, while the player from the second group showed the reflection the player had made about what was important in the exercise. But what brought me the most joy was to see between the lines that the 'why?' and 'what for?' had been questioned. This meant that the player internally had questioned themselves throughout and even understood. When the player said "in my case" it was already a decisive step. They spoke about it in the first person and had related it to the exercise. They talked about what they were learning and concluded how they were learning a lot through this exercise! This was the culture of learning!

Those were the years which I enjoyed watching and listening to the players, especially from the youngsters (10-11 years old) and the juveniles (16-17 years old), talking in first person, asking questions to the coach, explaining the exercises to their teammates, talking about their objectives and giving each other feedback. I had an increasingly clear conclusion: How much potential we lose from the player when we subject them to a learning framework based on 'I teach you and you do what I tell you, and I am the coach.'

The immediacy of the results and the need of control for coach seeks to simplify the complexity of learning in people, and when we simplify it we limit them.

It became increasingly clear to me that Javier Garcia de Andoin's statement that there were no shortcuts in player development was imbued within me and many of the coaches.

WHAT ARE THEY TALKING ABOUT?/WHAT IS YOUR MESSAGE?		
That the player faces up to new situations	We want the player to recognise their football difficulties	We want to see that they are capable of capturing a solution style against good teams

"OUR EVALUATIONS HAVE TO BE MADE FROM ANOTHER PERSPECTIVE"

The competition is the means to demonstrating the real performance of the player	The purpose is trying to maximise the style of our players, which will give all our teams an identity

(Edorta Murua, current Director of Football at the Aspire Academy & formally of Athletic Club Bilbao)

Edorta Murua summed it up in this sentence: *"In the end, it is a matter of identifying players, teams, coaches and managers alike by a way of dealing with situations with a set of values, a style, through our performance. That's where our identity lies."*

This learning period lasted about two years. The future of the first team and the advance of the elections would close one stage and open another one that would be much ruptured in terms of the culture we had been working with. Even so, the Department of Psychology tried to continue developing new and better learning scenarios.

CHAPTER 5
COACH-TO-COACH LEARNING
MENTORING. (2007-2011)

These were the years of impasse, years of reflection, of looking back and analysing the learning road travelled so that we could continue taking steps. Learning was to be the object of development. Even in our conversations with the players and coaches, the technical aspect carried more weight (Why don't you volunteer to speak? You have space to do so.), compared to the human (What part of me as a player is in danger if I volunteer to speak?).

We needed to evolve in the idea and meanings of learning, we needed to improve our interventions and conversations from conceptual to experiential learning. The player received good information within the conversations with the coach as they reflected on their actions and generated knowledge about the game, but were we getting to generate understanding about themselves in the game?

In general, and within the world of sport, the speeches on formation from the sportsman or woman demand that the players are creative, that they are able to think and make decisions, but often neither the structures nor the contexts change to be able to unfold that process. Therefore, we had to take that step.

What training contexts develop these psychological needs of the player?

To understand this, we propose the example of these two images. What do we see in the picture? In the black and white photo there are some workers doing a task, and always doing the same task. It's a mechanical job and they repeat the same movement continuously. They don't need to think. The task is only physical. Our teams often behave this way. The colour photo shows the workers moving and there is communication between them. They're sharing information and they're thinking together.

I'm sure both cases achieve good results. However, if we look around the world of football, which factory is best suited to the demands of the automotive industry or the world of football? Who would be more competitive? Many times, we ask players to have commitment, we want them to be responsible, and we want them to be motivated to overcome difficulties. From these two images, many questions arise that will serve as a reflection for the work we must develop as coaches and as trainers:

What kind of players are we creating in the black and white context? Where is the responsibility here? If something goes wrong in the process, no one would probably feel responsible, i.e. the problem is not mine.

What about the player's autonomy, their ability to make decisions, to take initiative, to find solutions to problems? Where's the creativity? Where is the learning here? Where is the development of the person who works in this factory? Do you use your talents? Which factory do you want to work in? What do you want for you and your players? What kind of leadership do you see in every picture? What skills does the leader need to create in the black and white context and which ones in the colour context? And by always moving it to football: Where are the most risks? Where is the leader that has everything under control?

We need coaches who have enough confidence to allow players to take risks. We need coaches who don't feel the need to control everything, all the time.

In which training styles does all this potential develop? The training style that develops talent, potential, that responds to their **needs has to be put into action**. It doesn't have to do with the 40 minutes of training, it doesn't have to do with preparing some exercises and executing them, nor with watching videos of the opponent, but with what we are doing to develop the player, *what spaces are we creating?* What are we doing to treat the player this way? **It has to do with how the coach lives it and where they live it from.** Neither the exercises, nor the videos, nor the planning develop that potential; **it is the type of coach-player relationship that makes it possible**. The educational process of talent development, has little say here, as there is a lot of interaction between the player and coach. More so, what one does in this educational process is to show oneself as the person they are and from there one grows. It is a two-way process. Therefore, the first step in being able to educate is to be able to expose myself as the person I am, for the other person to be able to see me and for me to see the other person. When I feel like I need the other person to help me grow, then I'm starting to feel like a coach/educator. In that process we know that the outcome is important but we also know that it is not the most important thing.

Any objective is built and built in a process, and what happens in that constructive process is what matters to us. We are interested in how we are implying that process and how we are building it. All too often we put our attitude at the service of the objective, and the important thing is the journey that the player-coach makes. The important thing is the processes, one that which we do not have to stifle with the urgency or immediacy of results, because there lies the possibility of transformation and creation. If the focus is only the result, it would be preparing us to understand a small corner of life.

At that time, the messages from the coaches were still directive, they said how and what to do, and we rarely heard questions or silences aimed at letting us think; the pre-match talks or performance criteria were focused from and for the scoreboard. The social paradigm of *"results are what matter"* is still very much anchored in all of our society.

After many years of working on player development, I have seen that it is said very quickly *"we want a player who thinks"*; however, this is a long and complex transformation process, which requires persevering leadership. This is not achieved by a talk from the coordinator at the beginning of the season, nor by forcing or coercing. If we want competitive players, we need to end the separation between those who think and those who do. The combination of the coach who thinks what needs to be done and a player who executes, did not serve us in Lezama, not for a very long time.

In Lezama, we needed to evolve from mechanistic learning (the player who obeys) to cognitive learning (the player who thinks). To this day, learning becomes a value for us and it is about getting the player to actively participate in their own learning. Empowering learning as opposed to teaching; therefore, it is not a matter of the coach coming in and saying what to do. The aim is for the player to learn to find the solution to the game's problems on their own, and to take responsibility for their learning and to reflect on it.

> *"The reality of football tells us that players must be prepared to face the situations that the game will present to them. A game that demands rhythm, intensity, speed, determination, but also control, balance, pause; in short, it demands understanding of the game. To understand the game you need to think about the game. We need players who think, who are **autonomous**, who un-*

derstand the game and who make decisions for themselves."

Edorta Murua

We had to end the separation between those who think (coaches) and those who obey and execute (players). From there, the following foundation was put in place and was the key to generating these learning spaces.

FIFTH FOUNDATION: INFORMATION VERSUS KNOWLEDGE

The distinction between information and knowledge defined a before and after in my work, and above all in my outlook.

"The player has to understand the game and its connotations," said Edorta Murua, who was then the person responsible for developing the players' and coaches' understanding of the game. Murua explained: *"The knowledge of the game is not learned in a staggered way or in pieces, but from the whole and as a result of multiple and diverse experiences within it."* Getting to know the game - and whatever it is - means learning, experiencing, and not buying a book or listening to long talks by coaches in the dressing room, because all that is just information.

I also learned that knowledge is not something that can be transferred, that it cannot be given as if I were giving you a glass of milk, that you take it and that's it. As the business consultant Maite Dárceles explains so well:

"There *is no automatic transference process of valuable and enriching experiences of wisdom; in short, it is a process of search and experimentation that everyone has to go through.*"[17]

Now we really had a problem. How many times have I heard these kinds of phrases?: *"I want to train to pass on my knowledge to the players", "we are going to bring in ex-players as coaches to pass on their knowledge and their experiences to the players".* All of this was just going to be information and information that for others had been valid, but that didn't have to serve our players twenty years later. At that time, I also learned that contexts change and so should the modes of intervention.

In my reflections, I concluded that the really relevant knowledge for our competitiveness is not the one we can listen to, read or see in the videos, but the one we can display from the heart of the game; that is, the knowledge that the player generates in action and in playing. Therefore, our interventions needed to be made from the very reality that emerges from the game and from what was happening. It was about

---

17   Guide to transformation – Hobest.

taking advantage of these situations within the game and then intervening from there. Doing this, rather than taking the player into a room and talking to them about motivation or overcoming adversity. Not only was the knowledge of the game beginning to emerge, but also the knowledge of myself as a player.

The first person foundation pillar was again relentless if we wanted to go deeper into the game and learn what happens to me, player or coach, within the game. This was aligned to the emotions, beliefs and the expectations that the players many times expressed about their performance on the field: *"I see the space, but I don't dare to pass"; "if I press to get the ball back, I get tired and then I can't attack."*

It is key to understand the knowledge gained from shared experiences. In our dialogues in the changing rooms we must generate knowledge and not just give pre-game information talks. Therefore, the key was to generate a learning context so that the player's knowledge could be displayed before or after their action; that is, to understand what was close to their reality, not to the reality of others, such as past experiences of coaches or anecdotes of former players. These past experiences and anecdotes are for another time, not to generate knowledge or self-knowledge.

"Knowledge happens as soon as it is stuck to reality. If it moves away it loses freshness, it loses

opportunity, it loses actuality; that is to say, it loses reality."

Maite Dárceles [18]

One question we asked ourselves back then was: **What do players learn: information or knowledge?**

The development of an autonomous and responsible player could not be done by means of information, which made a new step in the role of the coach and became an imminent requirement. Giving masterful talks at games, making directive corrections on what and how to do, giving great advice and solving the problems that the game poses to the player were already part of the past in the Lezama cantera.

We needed to continue and strengthen ourselves in generating new meanings as coaches, creating participatory training and moving from lectures to dialogue before and during the games; any excuse to reflect and share with each other was a good opportunity. Non-directive messages were replaced by questions, i.e. why and for what purpose do we do things?

The approach was clear, but a new question arose that helped us to continue creating our learning culture: What tools can help us in the process for generating a context that allows for autonomous players to grow?

---

18   Guide to transformation – Hobest.

So we built up our own **learning elements**, which appeared in our conversations with the players:

- To generate spaces for the player to reflect on their objectives, difficulties and achievements in training sessions and games. At 6:45 pm the locker room doors were closed; inside, the teams were talking and reflecting on what was coming up: objectives, emotions, exercises, games, the game and its principles.
- Self-knowledge, through dialogues in the dressing room and conversations with and amongst the players.
- Working with objectives.
- Enquiring questions, which the coaches would throw at the players in these spaces. As Javier Garcia de Andoin expressed in one of the courses that we organised with the Self Institute: *"The questions are the engine of learning, because they help to develop an interiorisation learning; the player is active in their learning, through the question we challenge the player to leave their comfort zone"*. If we were looking for **productive and mature learning**, this is developed by the process of internalisation rather than obedience and/or identification. This means that forming a **thinking and responsible player** would be created by questions of a reflexive type and by the participation of the player.
- Speaking in the first person singular. The aim is for the player to talk about themselves, to speak in

the first person of the singular, because we tend to talk about ourselves, about the team, and by using that plural the responsibility is blurred.

• Teach the player to give and ask for feedback.

• Challenge the player to challenge themselves. Talk to the players to challenge themselves, but not only about their actions but about what they think, because beliefs are what maintain our behaviours. If we want to change these behaviours, then we need to detect and unlearn beliefs that limit the player in achieving their goals.

• For me, this kind of conversation is what brings out the best in each player. It's a conversation that goes from the general to the concrete, from the superficial to the deep.

This line of work was more informal, there was no need for so many meetings, and we already had a framework and a common language. Many of the coaches were aware of their need to learn; including, where am I and where do I need to be as a coach?: conducting dialogues at games and in their management of training sessions; giving and receiving feedback. Even by doing all of this, we still needed to improve our questions, our intervention times and the quality of our conversations in order to generate the realities where the player was thinking, learning and becoming an expert on themselves.

Everything was made operational through the training and preparation by the psychologist. These were the years of much preparation on my part, of training in experiential courses (Transformation in the Organisations, Systemic Thinking, Organisational Constellations, Transpersonal Analysis), but above all my self-questioning was key. I was the one who had to evolve in listening, in asking and in deepening my learning. Only in this way could I model the questioning and the listening of the coach when I observed their dialogues in the locker room, educating my gaze, understanding and using my intuition, seeing what others did not see, listening to what was said and what was not said were several of my learnings in this process.

The approach was done, but I had to go a step further to make it practical: **How does this approach become operational?** This meant wanting to learn; for example, revealing myself to people who knew more than I did. You have to understand that working with people took me to my professional limits and that there was my opportunity to be a more complete professional. This cannot always be made operational if we are not willing to pay certain prices or understand these necessary vital growth pains.

MENTORING: MENTOR-MENTEE

A big step was taken at this stage. For a long time, I had in mind the importance not only of coaches being aware of their need to learn and to learn, but of learning together and in an autonomous way. On the other hand, it was necessary to leave this type of work of the institution apart from the people who were in it at that time. However, the great advances of these last years were the **feedback** between coaches and the **mentoring**.

There are probably many books on mentoring, but I didn't follow or look at any of them, as it just appeared as a need. New coaches were added, who realised that they needed help to follow the philosophy, methodology and learning processes of Athletic Club Bilbao. So, when a coach would say to me, *"How do I do this?"* or *"I don't understand the exercises"*, I first made them aware of the need to learn and the personal cost this entailed. It was a matter of showing the other person that I don't know everything and then offering them the possibility of asking a more senior coach. That's how I started to create alliances between coaches and naturally established this learning relationship between them.

The veteran coaches were great at this. They didn't approach it from the teaching side, but applied the same approach they had with their players, doing so by facilitating learning spaces through questions, feedback and, above all, understanding that the new coach learned from the old one, but the latter also learned from the new one.[19]

Feedback between coaches was another big step that emerged in these mentoring relationships. Asking for feedback from the player is relatively comfortable, but it was necessary to take another step since we are not used to asking for feedback from our colleagues, and even and why not, asking our bosses?

Over time, if you walked around Lezama after training sessions or games it was easy to hear how one coach would ask another for feedback on their performance in their training session or in their game. There was also regular first-person conversations that were not based on complaints or excuses but about the value or performance of players, or how the younger coach would ask the veteran to supervise their explanation of the training to the players. These mentoring processes meant that network learning was generated amongst the coaches.

In my conversations with the coaches, some of them, the older ones, told me how they had learned when they came to work at Lezama. You would come in the morning or before your training time and watch what and how other coaches did their work. You were learning in silence and solitude. Now ano-

---

19   Pablo Freire

ther way of growing up appeared and it had to do with learning from the coach: learning to learn between coaches, doing so through day-to-day interaction, sharing experiences and knowledge of trainings and competitions.

So, when a coach explained to me their difficulties in understanding training, for example, I suggested that we worked with another coach who was usually older than them on the project. The key was to build learning relationships, because not all relationships create learning. In these relationships, the first person, the questioning question, seeing further into the other person, and understanding their pace and moment in their learning process were some of the elements that could be heard in these mentoring conversations.

Over time, the young coach, who had been mentored by a veteran, grew up and accompanied new coaches. However, in turn these new coaches brought new looks, different processes that created different interactions and that also made the veteran coaches grow as mentors and as coaches.

This was shaping a learning network rather than a one-to-one relationship. Each node in the network was a coach who shared both moments: mentoring and being mentored. Learning spaces such as the dressing room, the moments before the training session, the game, post-training and post-games were no longer private spaces for the coach with their team, but became spaces shared by all coaches. If you watched a training from the outside, you could see the coach of the group that was training and another coach that was watching at an overview standpoint in order to learn or another coach that the first one had asked for feedback. Sometimes they had prepared the exercise together and then observed each other so that they could share that information.

You could also see them in the dressing room before training started or after the game. There was always a conversation about the game, but the content was no longer about complaints from the player or the team, but content about the player and their learning process, i.e. about whether the player had achieved their objective, whether there was improvement in them or not and, above all, if there was first-person reflection, what doubts the coach had, and what they had seen or not seen.

I remember one day I was listening to one of these conversations. The coaches were discussing a decision and everyone had their arguments. However, one of them raised a question: *"Where did you make that decision, thinking about your need or thinking about the player's need?"* The silence that was generated was wonderful, the coach's face changed, and there was the answer. It was in the change of look.

The coach thanked him and said, *"This question has been very helpful to me"*.

Little by little, the coaches understood the meaning of learning in Lezama, a non-instrumental learning that was not full of information, but a first-person and experiential learning. It was creating autonomy among them, and I no longer had to be facilitating those conversations, they could do it alone. Knowing how to withdraw from these spaces and take another place was another of the great learnings for me as a psychologist and I think that has been one of the most satisfying learnings I have had.

Mentoring was already well integrated into the Lezama cantera. One day I asked two coaches who had shared a mentoring process together to explain to me how they had experienced it. I asked the trainee coach to draw their line of learning from the time they had entered Lezama and to write down what the important milestones in this process had been.

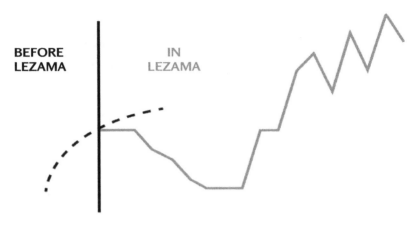

When I saw the line, I started to laugh. I was surprised even though I already knew it. It was the same as mine. The young coach told me about their process and their relationship with the mentor coach:

"When I entered Lezama I said to myself: I can't forget what I am. The beginning was about becoming aware of where I was coming from, a totally different club, and now my new context. Until then I thought my line was going to be upwards and growing. I thought if I was here it was because I was prepared for it. However, when my day started, I met the group that I would train. The players and the other coaches started the trainings and I saw how other coaches train, how they carry out their exercises with the group, and I start to doubt myself. I blocked out everything, I just read and said what it described on the sheet of paper. I doubted my ability and I wanted to fucking going home. One day I felt like I was hitting rock bottom".

libro
futbol
.com
AL GOL SE
LLEGA LEYENDO

This moment, the *feeling of touching* the bottom coincides with the bottom of the curve drawn. It's a delicate moment, because the coach has been divesting themselves of what they were bringing, of what they had been doing up until now, which had given them their results in other clubs and which had given them security above all. Not all coaches continue the line upwards, many unconsciously turn back. This is where you see that learning I'm talking about. This is an apprenticeship that shows you your limits, that invites you to enter into the unknown territory, which shows you your lights and your shadows; in other words, it is an apprenticeship in which I learn about myself. Not everyone is willing to make that awakening, because almost always it is painful.

This young coach told me: *"I learned to be in this situation. I was aware of my insecurity and the discomfort it brought. I began to be aware of my shadows and to accept them. I took steps. I understood the reason for the process, I also saw that there was another way. Not all the coaches followed this one, but I already saw what I wanted for me and what I didn't.*

There is a moment, perhaps at the end of the first year and the beginning of the second year that I said: that's it, I've learned everything. However, more complex situations appeared. This time I looked at them and faced them, but again I had doubts. They frus-

trated me, but this time I knew how to dialogue with them in a constructive way, I knew that they were my travelling companions and I needed to listen to them. I realised that I was growing again, and I watched my mentor build me up as a coach.

It was a path that I liked, that required my full self, which had its ups and downs. In turn, I looked for people I could approach and express my doubts. I was surprised no one was judging me by my questions or, for example, how I interpreted the football exercise. I felt heard and it wasn't a relationship of complacency. They didn't buy my excuses. They talked to me about process, but I didn't see it, I wanted results. The mentor left me space and I would look for him, I wanted to do it like he did already, but he didn't give me solutions, he returned questions.

One day, I realised that he was letting go of me, that he was at another distance from me. I thought, I'm not ready to do this alone yet. But I had a good run of results, and I said to myself, I have mastered this. It wasn't long before I took a hit. It was hard for me to accept that he was not there yet in this moment because he knew I need to deal with this moment on my own.

I remember that the mentor told me: "Snap out of it". On the other hand, he forced me to expose myself, I realised that he always listened to me. We talked more and more and I began to see his vulnerabilities as he saw mine. One day, he asked me to give him feedback on his training. How can I give you feedback if I don't know anything? I thought. But he insisted, and I realised that he's learning with me, too.

Here I understood what a learning relationship was. It was horizontality. It was from person to person, each one with their function, but both knew they were learning from each other."

Another important aspect that emerged was when the **Coach-Mentor** also told me about their experience in this relationship with the new coach they were mentoring:

"I knew what they were going through; I had lived it too, but I went through it alone. He would come in the mornings to watch the training sessions by coaches. This was time-consuming and he knew the philosophy well. In the first conversations I had with him I could already see that he was restless. I tried to make myself available to him and that he would come to me, but I would not seek him out or give him everything he asked for either; he would need to take the initiative. I listened to him, I didn't judge him, but I didn't buy the first thing he said either.

I saw that he was more unconstrained, more confident and I also saw that he was having a good run of results, I knew that he believed that everything was already learned and mastered. I could see that he was settling in and losing perspective. So I decided to wait.

The performance of his players will put him in his place, I thought. Then I would see him coming and look for my reinforcement and I wouldn't give it to him. But if I did return a question that made him think, I know it was making him uncomfortable. I was leaving him space so that he could look for me. I didn't do it all. Sometimes I could have given him solutions so that he wouldn't suffer, but I didn't because I trusted him. I knew he was going to take the big step and he did.

Eventually, I asked him to give me his feedback, too. I'd ask him to come and help me in the training sessions or in the dialogue with the players in the dressing room. I'd ask him to explain an exercise or give an opinion. I knew it was hard for him, but you learn by doing. We each found our own place and space. I felt that he was learning from me, but that I was also learning from him and I was letting him know it."

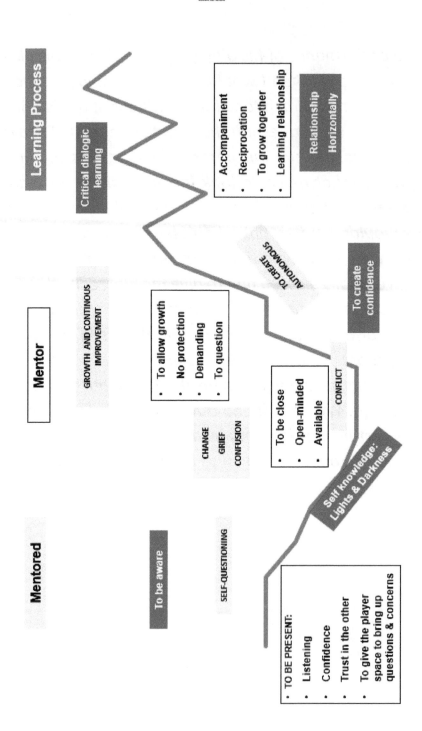

Jonatan Cabanelas, Coordinator Aspire Academy

Listening to him, I realised how much we had all learned. In his words the mentoring coach saw the importance of listening, trusting the other person, being present and being available to them. I saw the importance of distance management, just like in football: if I'm too close, I suffocate the other person and don't give them a chance to progress; if I go too far, I disconnect, then they don't see me. Manage distances according to the needs of the game, as coaches say. In this case it would be according to the needs of the trainee. Both were building real trust where being away from cronyism or protectionism, exposing each other, questioning and moving into unfamiliar territory were important foundations of that trust in the relationship. Finally, this learning relationship emerges, which starts as an accompaniment and ends up being a reciprocal growth with each other.

CHAPTER 6

THE ORGANISATION.

PARTICIPATION AND SHARED VISION (2011- SEPTEMBER 2013)

After all these years, we continued to question what we were doing and how we were doing it with the spirit of deepening, understanding and optimising the growth of the players. We still had to improve many aspects such as the use of questions or detecting the beliefs that limit the performance of players. It also meant improving the transmission of messages both at the verbal level and from within the physical body, although the great challenge was transmitting the emotional language. Questions we were working on amongst the coaches: Where do we say things from? What emotion do I speak or act from?

However, at this stage the focus of the intervention was evolving, in my view, because it was no longer just about understanding the game, but about understanding me as a player or a coach within the game. What happens to me as a player when I have the option to play on the inside or when I leave my position? How do I live this experience? That leads me to deepen my emotions and my emotions as a coach.

These were topics that were increasingly appearing in meetings and, as a consequence, the focus of the coaches' conversations with the players also changed. There was a shift from talking about the technical ("There's no space") to the emotional ("What do I feel when there's no space and what consequences does that have on my decision in the game?").

Moreover, football itself and the training process made us ask new questions:

• How do we deal with the increasing complexity of training the player?

• Can we teach to be a future player if we don't know the future?

• How do we football technicians live with and manage uncertainty?

• How do we wake the player up from their lethargy expressed in phrases like *"the coach doesn't give me confidence"* or *"the coach says"*?

libro
futbol
.com
AL GOL SE
LLEGA LEYENDO

103

In 2011, Jose Mari Amorrortu became the director of Lezama again. His proposal focused on achieving a deeper cohesion around the organisation's project. This implied the participation in the coherence of the philosophy for all who were part of it, from the youngest players (10 years old) to the second team[20], and of course to make this philosophy and teamwork reach all corners of the organisation.

In a club like Athletic Club Bilbao we can't stop walking forward. The next step was a great challenge, under the motto we are all part of Lezama and we are all Lezama. This was to strengthen the participation for everyone involved in the updating and evolution of the project so that it is something sustainable over time. This new collective organisational vision had to

20   Bilbao Athletic (second team), plays in the Spanish Second B or Second Division. Against senior professional teams.

be incorporated into the day-to-day working culture and an attempt was made to develop it through shared projects.

Working with projects means that a group of people get together to reflect and deepen their understanding of a topic. Finally, upon reflections, these have to be translated into one or two activities that have to be carried out.

During this period, we did two days of reflection that was outside our usual work environment. There were about fifty of us, and by using a SWOT analysis came several projects:

- identity and belonging project;
- communication project;
- learning project; and
- leadership project.

These projects represented the improvement needs for all of Lezama's professionals. Working groups were formed, and each group was responsible for a project and for organising the different activities to carry these projects out.

Several visits were made to other organisations. We were in an organisation that stands out for its leadership management and to complement this we moved to a teaching system by the University of Mondragon, which stands out for its learning, and was based on the Finnish educational model.

The coaches who made the visit to the University of Mondragon had to educate the rest of the people within the Club about this particular education system. Everyone chose their own way to explain this system by also trying to promote participation and learning. Workshops, presentations and other activities were organised. The aim was to make us aware of the generating knowledge and that this knowledge would emerge from these shared experience by the interaction of critical and creative thinking.

Internally, this learning project had set meetings that would give people the possibility for someone from the organisation to explain about their learning experience or other related topics. This led to the management of the academic subjects for all the players being improved. An update was made on the studies of the players, where they studied and any problems or needs that they had.

We connected with the schools with the idea of being closer to them, getting to know them and getting them to know us. We attended to cases of players that had study problems and included reading in our daily life. The youngest and infantil players (10 to 13 years old) had a reading workshop every month. The aim was to make us aware that with a philosophy like ours, whose foundation is in education, is a collective task that implies generating knowledge about oneself and about the context in which we were living as an organisation. Shared experiences continued to contribute to this.

However, this did not bear all the fruits desired at first. Perhaps we were not prepared as an organisation for such an ambitious change. Although during these years, the working groups met in an autonomous way and developed the objectives of the project, by ending with a plenary meeting where the results were shared. I realised that it was one thing to do a project and another different and bigger thing to change the culture of an organisation. This couldn't be done just by applying techniques so we had a long way to go in this endeavour.

This experience of living through the projects led me to initial reflections, which should be the starting point of any process of change. In my experience, the traditional model of education and management has fallen. These more hierarchical paths (where one thinks and the others execute, where one hears little). We already know what kind of player it leads to, but for many it is and has been their way of working. Changing the concept of work, of training, of seeing the development of the player means breaking down many beliefs and above all it means going out of our comfort zone. Not everyone is willing to take this trip.

I'm not talking about methodologies, player profiles, structures, planning and pre-established routes. I'm talking about a way of seeing the formation of the person within football. More so, that allows this person to develop their full potential and acquire the necessary maturity in terms of autonomy and responsibility to face the future of the game. This change cannot be forced, it has to come from the desire of each one. Desire is an exciting vision of the future. This generates dissatisfaction with the present and drives more challenging and desirable purposes. However, as always, that change has to be from the inside out.

It is a long and complex working process with comings and goings, but as in almost all cases, it is the people who have made and make it possible or impossible.

CHAPTER 7

LIGHTS AND SHADOWS DURING THE LEARNING

(SEASON 2012-13)

Throughout all these years, there was clarity in the **What** we wanted to do. We asked ourselves what the player needs were, what appears in the processes during the formation of the player and what was missing in them gave us the **How** to carry it out. Above all, the imperative need to take care and educate the person who deploys those **Whats** and those **Hows** and put them at the service of the person **Who** receives them.

At that time, we had a basis for action with a clear and defined objective, but further reflection was needed. What orientations and guidelines are underpinning and supporting this new reflection?

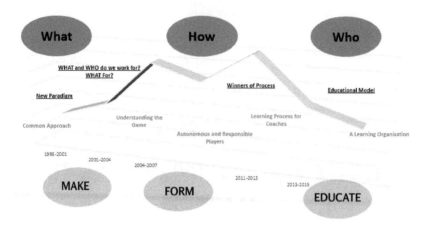

Edorta Murua, María Ruiz de Oña, Vicente Gómez

- Lezama couldn't be everybody's dresser drawer. Like every school, it must have an educational plan that is not dependent on teaching implementations from the outside. Its training implementations need to be based on the educational model and learning philosophy of that school, in this case the school of Lezama. The tools we use have to be appropriate for this school.

- Education is practice, the rest is demagogy. The kind of actions we bring into play in our interactions have to do not only with technical competence, but also with personal competence. Therefore, Lezama's coaches develop actions with their players that affect both the professional and personal environment.

- The results of the learning process cannot only be assessed from the point of view of results (competition), because these are the product of something external and, as such, instrumental, but must also be analysed. As priority, they need to be from the point of view of processes, because it is within these processes that difficulties are encountered. These difficulties will have to be worked on in the here and now so that the result is satisfactory for all.

• Working with an educational perspective in high competition sports does not alter the product, either in terms of efficacy or results, what alters is the product of being more of a person or being less of a person.

• Our experience is that players who have grown up in these contexts go much further, either by creativity, by construction or by feeling like a person; from other perspectives, we have seen them fall at the first sign of change.

FUNDAMENTALS

When we are talking about integrated training and comprehensive education. What did we mean by this?

• Psychological training and learning must have a place and time in practice sessions and games, because they are part of them.

• We are training and educating the player, but the one who sustains that player is themselves. Not to develop the person inside this player is to limit oneself.

• We work on tactical intelligence and cognitive intelligence. However, we need to understand better how to integrate the emotional intelligence and to greatly improve the overall collective intelligence (talent) in both players and coaches.

• To comprehend the theoretical frameworks on which the area of psychology and learning are based are on, among others, critical pedagogy and humanist psychologies. These are based on the need for the participation of the player in his/her learning. That he/she be an active and responsible subject in the process in order to achieve a vital, sustainable learning and development of the player's person.

LIGHTS AND SHADOWS

From the first day that I entered to work in the Lezama cantera, my questioning of the presence of the psychologist, of my approach and understanding of what was happening there had been with me. After a few years, this self-reflection was gaining strength and greater presence. At that time, there were a series of facts and situations that invaded my gaze and that hijacked my questions; in short, there were issues that, of course, had grown, but were falling into instrumentalisation, into functionality, forgetting their ethics, who are they are they at service of, their aesthetics, and the intentionality with which we approached the player. All of this worried me a lot and these were some of my observations:

- I am not sure that we are aware, that we are awake in our learning process.
- Do we really understand what learning is?
- We need to create more spaces for collective learning, formal and informal.
- We're standing in a process of self-awareness with the coaches. I sense it in conversations. What do we talk about when we do it in the first person singular? If we look, many first-person conversations are in a loop, a pattern that repeats itself. What parts of me are repeated in my conversations?
- First-person leadership (stop being a victim of circumstances and actively participate in creating new circumstances)
- Learning in the first person (how am I as a coach, as an apprentice?).
- The language of emotions is difficult for us to handle, some by excess, some by default.

I perceive a stagnation in the key processes: As seen below, these key processes are sometimes used according to our needs and not the needs of the player.

- Questions are key to the learning process. I can't ask what I can't answer. We need to get better at asking questions.
- Sometimes our needs (limitations) as coaches are hidden behind these key processes and tools.
- These key processes are not substitutes for our skills as coaches, we have to continue to deepen our skills as coaches; otherwise they will become tools to be used and thrown away. If there is no process of self-knowledge and personal work of the coach, these tools cannot be understood. It is through the experience in oneself that we understand them.

I felt that another step had to be taken. In all these years, I was very aware that we had not brought any external professional to Lezama to help us broaden and deepen our outlook. These were years when coaching was very fashionable and coaches came to Lezama to present projects, all of them very respectable, but far from being able to respond to the level of reflection that we had reached in these years amongst the players and coaches. I was trained in coaching by one of the few approved schools in Spain. During that time, there was such a flood of projects and offers that I decided to train myself and in this way know confidently what exactly coaching is, while also having the knowledge to respond to these projects and offers as best as possible.

One day I was called to participate in a conference on Coaching and Sport organised in Bilbao by the Association of Entrepreneurs. There I met Marcos Mansur. I remember that he approached me after the event to tell me: *"You said that listening has been your best school for your learning, you talked about listening".* Then I realised that Marcos was talking to me about a listening that even I was not aware of, a listening that went beyond the active listening that appears in the coaching manuals.

That day was a before and after in my professional career. Marcos invited me to Self Institute, a place where even the concept of entering transmitted something different. There I met Javier García de Andoin, whom I thank and will always thank for all he has shared with me. Working with Javier was a giant step. It led to an awakening in terms of me and my knowledge. I shared many hours with Javier and Marcos. We had meetings to reflect on great themes, and I collaborated with them in their dialogues on vital learning and intuition. I thought that these people could really help us grow in Lezama. They were different from all the training businesses there was and is around football clubs. I spoke to Jose Mari Amorrortu so that he could meet them and give me the go-ahead for a meeting with them and the coaches.

Together with the Self Institute and Pilar Ruiz de Gauna[21] we organised two courses. The first is entitled *Learning in the Coach-Player Context from an Educational Perspective*. The approach of this workshop was based on two significant keys: one referred to the object of study on which we were going to investigate the coach-player interaction in its main key of learning, and the other referred to the method, the reflection on the action that is developed in a context of dialogue. This method is characterised by the sharing with others about personal experience that are impregnated with knowledge, beliefs, prejudices, theories, values. It is in this exchange that we contrast and question our own beliefs and those of others and it is in this act of interaction that people can acquire new understandings. This allows us to understand ourselves in the world and project ourselves in actions from these new understandings and, therefore, in a different way.

This process of building new understandings to address actions required a thoughtful process. In order to begin this journey, we proposed to investigate together the following questions:

• What is understood in Lezama by educational context? What lessons are being learned?

---

21   Pilar Ruiz de Gauna. PhD in Pedagogy from the University of the Basque Country.

- What elements are present in the coach-player interaction?
- What are the lights and shadows in the learning we do at Lezama?

RESEARCHING OUR EDUCATIONAL CONTEXT

The first question that came up was **whether we felt like educational agents or not**. Possibly, not all the people in the group could give the same answer to this question. As Pilar Ruiz de Gauna said, *"Some will think that they are educational agents and will try to work from there; others will think that a high performance school has to prepare its players from the technique and leave aside 'that other thing', because there is no time for everything. While others will think that education is a family thing and that the player has to come with it from home"*.

Perhaps, this way of expressing and living this experience has been built from individuality and it is necessary to think globally as an institution in order to act locally as a coach. From this premise, we entered into a second question concerning the institution: What is the training project of the School of Lezama? What does the institution want the players to learn? What is your common project? Is it something implicit? It is something explicit with which we dialogue and improvement actions are established?

If we wanted to work along the lines of rethinking this institutional framework, it was necessary to stop and reflect on what our players were learning and the actions we were taking together to develop this project. Surely, if we were to review the type of actions that we put into play in our interactions, we would observe that many of them have to do not only with technical competence but also with personal competence.

Therefore, we closed this particular subject by noting that Lezama's coaches developed actions with their players that affected both the professional and personal spheres. Furthermore, we still left open the initial question of whether we should consider ourselves as educational agents. Each one would have to generate knowledge about this point throughout the workshop, although we knew that this was not something that could be left to the whim of each one of us. It required a greater understanding of the context in which we found ourselves and it needed a collective and institutional response.

To generate this understanding of the context, it was necessary to ask ourselves if the spaces of interaction that were given between coach-player on the field, dressing room, etc., were characterised as an **educational context**. These contexts are potential

spaces of interaction (action between people), created intentionally so that the coach/educational agent
and the player acquire a series of learnings (professional and personal), and become aware of their situation within the world and the direction that their
action should take. This context is characterised by
the presence of communicative action or dialogue
and certain situations must be preserved: that we are
all treated as people, with dignity and with respect,
that we can share our experiences under equal conditions, even if we are occupying different roles, and
that we can express ourselves freely, from respect
and without fear of reprisals.

It is in this context of interaction that we had to place **the learning process** and it is in this context that
we needed to question how we were placing ourselves as coaches. This question should also include the
following: How do players position themselves in this
process?

Thinking about educational contexts in which the
focus is on learning means changing the very processes in which we have socialised ourselves, and have
more to do with the teaching-learning paradigm. This
is where the one who knows is placed in a hierarchical way in front of the one who does not know, while understanding the person as a reservoir that has
to be filled in order to reproduce what we transmit.
However, focusing on **learning and on the person/**

persons who learn leads to placing the coach-player in a horizontal and person-person relationship. In this interaction, the coach's question is not what do I have to teach and how will I do it? but what does the player have to learn?, how will you learn it?, and how are you going to show me that you've learned it? In this framework, it is when coach and player become co-responsible for the training process, with the player taking the leading role within it.

If we focus on the player, our next step should be to ask ourselves what we need to learn in order to achieve an autonomous player who is mature enough to face life in high-performance football. We highlighted the following as possible significant competencies of the player:

1. To have a technical knowledge built from critical thinking.

2. To work on finding solutions to the situations that arise.

3. To handle uncertainty and give creative answers.

4. To make decisions and assess the consequences of their actions.

5. That the player is motivated to continue learning and developing personally and professionally.

If these are the competences that the coaches have to develop in the players, then new reflections arrive: What kind of strategies did we have to develop to reach these learnings? What are the learning environments to be like? Where were we promoting all this?

These were some of the questions that the group raised in that unforgettable workshop. Furthermore, in this workshop and the next one we introduced, thanks to Javier Garcia de Andoin, the body in the context of learning, that is to say, body intelligence, something I always had in mind, but didn't develop in Lezama.

I remember that we started this particular session by paying attention to the importance of making our bodies aware as being one more element of communication. In this sense there was talk of body intelligence and the body as an element of interaction with our players.

At all of these sessions we started with exercises that helped to unfold the knowledge that the body has and that we are almost always unaware of. After that, we were silent as a form of collective learning arrangement. We differentiated between being silent and being quiet. Silence is a conscious and active position. Then, the coaches in the group were invited to express what they had realised while performing the exercise. The question we asked ourselves was: Is our body in a listening position when we interact with others? In turn, we experience the restorative effect of working with the body. *"The body is our great for-*

gotten," I remember Javier Garcia de Andoin telling us.

We concluded the course with many questions, as is typical of the courses I shared with the Self Institute. For example, how do I realise that I've learned? How do I put what I learn into action? Why is it important today, in the here and now, to talk about learning?

Two models of learning emerged that lead to two paths with each one taking us to different places:

1.   The learning path looks outside to the outside, it looks at the norm, to apply techniques, models to what I am putting outside of me. Or that of the one who builds me from the outside with the values that are outside. The movement of this learning is from the outside in. There has to be rules, but what are those rules in the service of? What is their function? How are we assessing its effectiveness?

2.   This learning path looks from the inside out. Something inside me is disturbing, questioning, or needs to be understood. It is a learning that generates understanding, it is the learning in which the action starts in oneself to then go outside through dialogue, interaction, questioning, feedback, and from the outside it returns inside to oneself by generating understanding and knowledge in the first person and to be able to apply it in the following actions that are presented to us.

"Am I taking the person out of learning or am I understanding from and for the learning?" Pilar Ruiz de Gauna asked us.

So, what are we talking about when we talk about learning? **Learning for training or learning for education?** Am I training or educating? Where do I place myself in oneself and the other person? What does learning for training mean? It means **instrumentalising** someone else to get something and then what I'm doing to me is also instrumentalising myself. Furthermore, doing what I tell you, using the person for the benefit of another and what you are building is not for them, it is for the benefit of others.

Javier Garcia de Andoin continued: *"This place of learning is a vulnerable place, to educate is to always place oneself in a place of extreme fragility. Against that, there appear the formulas that are not educational (leitmotifs, positive psychology, misused coaching, second hand ideas, banner slogan ideas) that do not transform anything, do not create anything and hinders a lot.*

In front of this, there is dialogue, critical thinking, personal reflection, interaction with the other person, and respect and listening. In an organisation you have to know what responsibility and place we have, and if you don't see it, you have to start educating yourself.

Can one commit 100% from that fragile and vulnerable place? Is there a safety floor? Can there be an anchor that gives us the certainty that this commitment is not always subject to permanent doubt? This is where we're putting the focus? What are we committing to? What does this mean for everyone?

Education cannot be secondary, so we have to learn to have this gaze and viewpoint. Creativity is something else. Talent is something else. It is an innate quality and it only flourishes in spaces that humanise, in spaces that are built from humanisation. To educate is to humanise."

In that course we learned something that opened our eyes and gaze to all of us: education is a process of humanisation; the problems come when it stops being so. And what does that mean? The dilemma is that if we put ourselves in the position of dehumanisation, if I am not humanising what I am doing is dehumanising. We would never forget this.

The second course focused on *reflecting on leadership and teams.* Here we were accompanied, in addition to Javier García de Andoin and Marcos Mansur, by Iñigo Echevarría, a questioning, pragmatic and humane man from the world of banking. They led us to take a step in the understanding of these great concepts and again broaden and deepen our view.

In the previous course we had reflected on how to establish educational processes in the coach/player relationship. We generate knowledge about what education is and what instruction is. We defined education as a process of humanisation and we understood that for this it is necessary to establish interaction between people, always from person to person and not from person to object.

This second course gave emphasis that this educational action must always be led by a person; that is, it is important to recognise myself in how I am developing this leadership, from where I am developing this leadership, or what is preventing me from exercising this leadership. Leadership emerges from one's own passion and from the conviction of my ideas and my actions. Doing so with a dose of authenticity, by having confidence in me and in the other person and managing my emotions and the conflicts that arise from the complexity of human relationships. In this process we must also recognise the value of the other person.

We also saw that in this leadership there are shadows: some are within ourselves (fear, mistrust, lack of conviction or vision, lack of commitment) and other times they are from outside us (lack of recognition of the institution, institutional power conflicts).

One possible conclusion we came to was: a leader who has passion conveys passion; a leader who has love conveys love; a frustrated leader conveys frustration. Both courses helped us to understand more, to deepen our daily action, gave us self-knowledge and strengthened our commitment to our reason for being in Lezama. For me it was something unforgettable.

From there, outlines of reflections that were needed when developing an educational project in a football club with a philosophy focused on developing players emerged.

EDUCATION AS THE FOCUS OF THE PROJECT 2013-14

Educating covers the entire global strategy of accompanying the player in their training. Doing so from an educational perspective that provides axes of personal growth based on a holistic idea of the person. This is where personal growth and sports are indivisible facets of the same development.

Responsibility, autonomy and learning are values that are enhanced in this process through critical dialectical learning, which we can base on reflection on action.

The matrix of our model was oriented to the **professional development of the coach**. This was a *sine qua non* condition[22] for the formation of a conscious and a mature player which were all key aspects of being a competitive player. Our reason being is the training of the player had all its complexity, dynamism,

---

22   Sine qua non is an indispensable and essential action, condition, or ingredient. It was originally a Latin legal term for "[a condition] without which it could not be".

and was framed in a performance-oriented participatory and self-critical learning culture with a winning attitude.

In this way, we were able to outline some key concepts to the Learning Model that were growing in Lezama and that were structured in the following way.

I. FUNDAMENTALS:

1. Educate and Learn

We feel educated to the extent that we consider education as the process where people's potential is developed.

Educating is a collective task. The Lezama collective is clear that the player is our value and that this value has to be **put into action**. That is, this value has to appear in **what we are doing to develop the player and in the spaces we are creating**. We are aware that situations arise where we leave training aside because we are distinguishing that what is important is the person.

In our reflection on what learning is, we concluded that **learning** is not only about scoring goals, but also about:

• **understanding**, giving meaning to what I do and **understanding myself** (as a player or coach), how do I feel? and how am I living it?

• to build ourselves from the **commitment and responsibility** to improve what we do. To transform oneself to become the best professional we can be and to transform the context where we are so that it becomes a space of learning and continuous development.

2. Training and competition are educational contexts.

1.   We consider training and competition to be an educational contexts where the focus is on learning and the people who learn.

2.   As a learner, we highlight the following **significant player competencies**:

• To have a technical knowledge built from critical thinking.

• To work on finding solutions to the situations that arise.

• To handle uncertainty and give creative answers.

• To make decisions and assess the consequences of their actions.

• That players and coaches is motivated to continue learning and developing personally and professionally.

3.   **The spaces of interaction between coach-player** in Lezama (training field, dressing room, etc) are the axis of this model and are characterised by the

educational context. In this space of interaction the following has to be present:

- Horizontal relationship, person-person (subject-subject).
- Communicative action or dialogue as a tool for self-knowledge and development of collective talent.
- Learning, which is based on the need for the active participation and awakening of the player in their learning; seeing the importance of the coach-player interaction for this. So, the question for the coach is not what do I have to teach and how will I do it? but what does the player have to learn, how will they learn it and how will they show me that they have learned it? And a final link is to know where the player can develop their creative capacity to intervene and understand the challenges of their personal and sporting life.

4.   It is within this framework that the coach-player becomes **co-responsible for the training process**, with the player taking the leading role within it.

3. The Coach is an Educator

Our educational model **integrates the professional development of the coach** so that they recognise and integrate these key competencies into their work and, from there, act as a creative force in the trainings and competitions.

Although there were psychological and educational tools in daily action that promoted learning, the point is that these alone are not enough to solve the challenges of learning. Like any instrument, these tools need a conscious user, capable of applying them effectively and able to adjust to the particular and concrete situation they face.

At Lezama, we believe that our competencies as coaches are based on **self-knowledge, on the effectiveness of interactions and on the maturity of our actions**.

4. The Physical Trainer is an Education Agent

The physical trainers, including the sport science staff and the other football club technicians that are involved in preparing the player physically must be aware of their educational action. These essential people have an educational task to implement into the player so that the player is aware of the necessity of training in order to be able to face the demands of the training sessions and games.

These physical trainers need to convey why and what we do they work for. The players must understand:

- the meaning of physical preparation.
- the importance of repairing physical deficiencies.

• the invisible training (i.e. the physical training that the player often has to complete on their own especially when recuperating from an injury).

Just like the football coach, the physical trainer creates spaces to receive and give feedback, spaces in which they teach how to generate healthy habits and an issue as important as the player learning to listen to their body. From the physical preparation we can create an important reflection for the player that is being formed: how would I be if I took care of my body? What would it be like to compete without that backpack?

In addition, there is the need to educate respect for the supplied physical material as part of the player's personal growth.

5. The Medical Service is an Education Agent

Explain the recovery process (diagnosis and treatment). We highlight key elements in the educational space that occurs in the interaction between medical service personnel and the player: *The aid; Duelling process.*

• The aid is seen as a process that teaches us to recognise what this educational space is and to not resort to false supports. Additionally, it is one that collaborates to develop and express the potential of each one.

• Our educating role here is far from psychological ploys where people adopt different positions (saviour, victim, protagonist) and to be aware that these roles can also be generated between patient and doctor or patient and physiotherapist.

• Duelling process: These medical encounters are a very important moment for a player, especially regarding the formation of the player. In the process of grief (i.e. in the case of getting an injury), we recognise two moments that we as professional educators want to distinguish in our daily medical practice:

  • During the stage when the person needs to regain strength, feel comforted, understood and sustained; this is not the time to see their responsibility or to respond with efficiency and lucidity. Right now, closeness is invaluable. Strengthen.

  • Or yet, during another point in the process, where caring, relieving pain, and comforting has the opposite effect: the development moment weakens, the person falls asleep, shields themselves and avoids taking the step. In these cases, relieving the pain and the discomfort takes away what it has of its power: that is its transforming power.

II. Horizon:

A series of strategies and elements that must characterise our teaching-learning processes in training and games must be present in the interaction between the coach and the player.

We start from a teaching-learning process that is generally more linked to the instructional than to the educational. This has to do with the processes in which we have socialised and which are more related to the teaching-learning paradigm where the one who knows is situated in a hierarchical way in front of the one who does not know. Understanding the person as a deposit that has to be filled in order to reproduce what we transmit.

Our focus now is on the question that the coach needs to ask themselves. This question is not so much related to what should be taught but what the player needs to learn. It is in this process that the coach also becomes an active part of their own learning and becomes a facilitator of the learning processes. From there the coach learns as a person and as a professional and in addition, they must master or learn a series of new skills to develop this education.

What must the coach's competencies be for this interaction to be truly educational?

We discovered in the process that in this interaction both **cognitive intelligence** and **body and emo-**

tional intelligence must be present. All of this is mediated by the dialogue.

a. Where is the emotion in the coach/player relationship?

In first-person learning. We mean everything that happens to me: where am I, what is happening to me, and how do I relate to what is happening to me? We want the player to realise their ability to intervene and understand the challenges of the moment. We want both the player and coach to understand the multiple learning possibilities that exist in their immediate reality.

Trust is the key part in this emotional field because it builds a floor of safety for different reasons:

• This is what has to sustain the professional responses of our players and us as coaches.

• We see trust as a space that creates a possibility, although that possibility is not in saying "I trust you" or "I trust me".

• For us, trust is related to the space that one opens up to be able to understand, to generate a context from horizontality, which has to do with being present and available to the player's needs and to listen to them without prejudice. There has to be a dialogue as a tool of self-inquiry.

But building trust is not a simple matter, and we must address a number of **keys to building that trust:**

1.   **Self-Knowledge:** If I cannot really connect with what is happening to me, it will be very difficult for me to understand what is happening to you.

2.   **Comprehension:** Confidence has to do with the ability of reading comprehension. Trust has to be able to build spaces so that you can learn, so that you can walk beyond that place of your shadows, blind spots, and mistakes; then you not only create a state of trust, but you create an environment that generates it.

3.   **Active attitude.** Trust is built, it is not a commodity to be given and taken.

4.   **Entering the territory of not knowing from my shadows and blind spots:** Trust allows me to learn from my limits as a coach and from yours as a player. In order to grow we must understand very well what our blind spots are, our areas that are in the shadows, and our vulnerabilities, because that is precisely what has to grow.

5.   **Recognise the person's resources and empower them**.

6.   **Listening and Dialogue.** In this sense, the coach is the one who has to generate the contexts of listening and dialogue.

b. Where is the cognitive intelligence in the coach/player relationship?

In understanding. When we have moved from information to knowledge, then the next step is to move from knowledge to understanding. The movement to know is different from the movement to understand. When we talk about understanding, we are talking about broadening our consciousness as understanding is an action that commits me, because I have to be present to the understanding.

c. Where is the body intelligence in the coach-educator relationship?

This is a further step, because we need to be aware of our body as another element of communication. There are a number of key aspects that will help us to improve communication in which body intelligence is involved:

1. **In the vertical gesture.** It seeks to be aware of my verticality in walking. To be vertical means to be **present** in the space, to be present in the step when walking, and without the head being elsewhere by the thought taking you out of this moment. This **verticality** that we express with the body is to **be available** to whatever arises.

2. **In the sensations of contact.** The coach's corporality must be highly present in the contact, where

the active attitude both in the movement of guiding and letting me be guided must be present in the coach and player.

3.   **Safety field.** This body work allows us to explore our movement, and both the coach and the player must explore new movements and be more open; that is, making the moment that takes us out of our safety field.

III. STRATEGIES:

In the teaching and learning processes we have to deploy a series of strategies that help us to develop these processes:

1.   **First-Person Learning**. As a first way of learning. We mean everything that happens to you by answering the questions: Where am I? What's happening to me? How do I relate to what's happening to me?

2.   **The question**. We build interaction through questions.

3.   **The feedback**. The other person acts as a mirror for us. We know that without the other person, we cannot learn.

4.   **Listening**. It has to be comprehensive and complete.

5. **The dialogue**. As a tool for self-knowledge.

6. **The coach-player interaction** is the space where we place the learning.

IV. ACTIONS:

Within our model, we must examine what the actions are in the different areas to find out what is being done and what our practices are like. The following were and still are actions that we consider important for the coach and player:

Actions with the players:

• Dressing room dialogues before training sessions and games.

• The players are protagonists and participate in the preparation of the training sessions and games.

• Self-management spaces: the players are left alone to prepare the training sessions and games.

• Feedback from the youngest teams in Lezama cantera (10-11 year old players) with the infantil (12-13 year old players). For example, the youngest players (10 years old), were in the changing room listening to the players who were 12-13 years old preparing the game and then giving these players feedback.

• A Basconia player from the third senior team (18-19 years old) attends and participates in the team dialogues before the games with the youngest players (10-11 years old).

• Meeting between the players at your request, with the idea of setting objectives, both individually and in groups.

• Training preparation of the youngest teams (10-11 year old players) with the juvenile B team (16 year old players).

• Anonymous tournament feedback from the players to the coach.

• Two teams come together to listen to each other, watch the competition and at the end share feedback between them.

• WhatsApp is used as a means of communication and learning.

• Players are encouraged to give each other feedback, without going through the coach.

• Non-football dialogue topics are encouraged and provoked.

Actions with the coaches:

• Training for the coaches (courses with Self Institute and internal training).

• Mentoring processes between the coaches.

• We have a learning network, where we accompany each other in our development as technicians.

- The coaches share the same training spaces, help each other, and listen to each other in their dialogues with the players, and then talk about what they have seen.
- Giving and asking for feedback is a common exercise in Lezama.
- We create work groups to improve the organisation through three projects and, in addition, we have made a project to improve the study habits:
  - communications project;
  - learning and leadership project; and
  - roles and functions project.

CHAPTER 8
CLOSURE.
(2015-2017)

Where do we come from? Where are we? These were the years of ordering, updating, validating or simply throwing away many of the elements that had been my companions on my journey through Athletic Club Bilbao. I could sum up these almost 21 years in this little picture, a picture which has evolved as well. In this picture are a collection of the many posts in which I had to stop and refuel in order to continue: the learning in first person, the player as a value, the change of leadership with coaches, the autonomous and responsible player, educating, the organisation that learns, developing the gaze, etc. These posts all opened up paths that I'm still walking today.

It was a common journey with a common language. The philosophy that the Lezama cantera had recon-sidered in 1997 meant that for years we were deepening and giving it content. Learning evolved from mechanical learning to vital, first-person learning that takes you to your limits, and that generates understanding and knowledge. The lucidity for some of the coaches made them realise that they needed to learn and change in this respect, and above all, the willingness to learn together by mentoring. All of this, accompanied by a continuous reflection of the training methodology. This included the understanding of the game by everyone, giving it a style of play, to have an improvement in the quality of training and, consequently, an improvement of the coaches.

In turn, in every light is its shadow and we had them too. There was a lack of shoring up and with the internalising of certain themes. For example: if the player has a problem, I am also part of that problem; the player's evolution speaks of my evolution as a coach; the player was solving experiential problems of the game, but were having trouble solving these problem within the game. Therefore, internalising what they had learned was something that had to be improved at all levels. On the other hand, there was movement in the organisation again, many of the coaches who had worked with me were leaving the Club and new ones were coming in. We were able to give continuity to some processes while others needed to start from scratch which meant adapting to the learning pace of these new coaches.

As time went by a group of coaches came to me with the concern to review and update the teaching and learning processes that we were experiencing. I found it very interesting, as many of them had not participated in the workshops we had done on learning, so I was sure it was going to help us in their understanding.

We had doubts as to whether or not the player was internalising everything they were learning in Lezama. Sometimes we feel like that's it, that the player has realised something and starts doing it, it seems like they have already learned and they're going to do it forever. However, the reality tells us that this is not the case. Sometimes we find moments of regression. *"They seem to have forgotten everything,"* said one coach. Or when in moments of impasse, *"This player has stalled,"* said another.

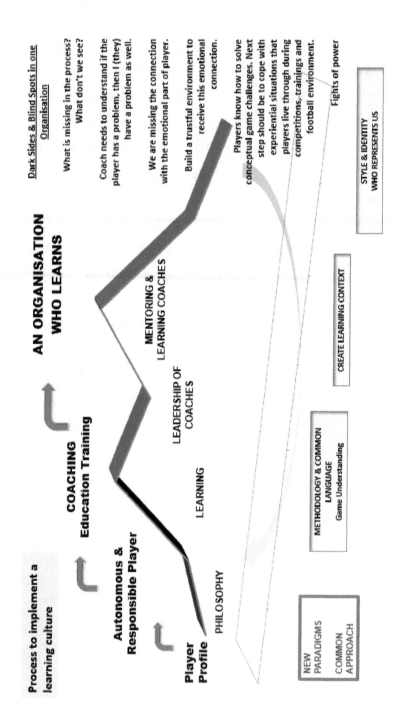

Edorta Murua, Football Head Director in Aspire Academy

Taking some distance, I listened to the coaches and saw their frustration behind these comments. I saw this linear thinking that most of us come from based on "I say and the player does it" or that illusion of cause-effect that creates unrest. However, few things are linear in life, let alone learning.

In the training courses for coaches I usually ask them to draw their line of learning. Most draw an ascending line and others a line with slight ups and downs. But only a few that draw the line with ups and downs will have backward and forward strokes or with looping circles.

Learning is not something linear but rather re-trogressive; that is, one step forward and one step backward, and it is the moments of regression that are the most important for the next step to be one of progression. However, these regressive moments need to be seen and understood as part of a process and, above all, must be invested in. The immediacy, the need to see *'the work done'* by coaches and the clubs, the fear of results or premature judgments, all add together to make us make decisions that break with this learning.

The regression or the impasse are moments that invite us to stop and look, and to think and question what is happening. These are good moments to reflect on my work as a coach, on what the player needs and what they need from me. These are spaces of great learning not only for the player but for the coach and even for the organisation.

So we looked again at some considerations that might help improve the internalising of the player's learning.

HOLISTIC APPROACH

To improve the internalisation process then we need more than a performance approach, we need to work from a deep and conscious learning process from which the player's development is enhanced. **A holistic approach that integrates the whole person**.

We cannot forget that under the player's jersey, there is a person who cannot be divided into technique, tactics, physical preparation, psychology, physiology, biomechanics, etc. The approach to the player must be global and integrated. It is imperative that the person does not break; that is, **that the player does not become divorced from their development as a person**.

In order to do so, educating the coach's gaze to look at the player that is beyond what they show on the field was one of the key challenges both from the methodology of football in Lezama and from the coach's learning proposal.

On the other hand, how many times do we hear: *"This player has made it to the first team because I saw them and brought them in,"* or other times this success is attributed to a particular coach?. From my point of view, these isolated performances alone would never generate a professional player or a sustainable performance over time. **I see performance as an emergent property**; that is, **performance arises** from the interaction of all the parts involved in it: the player themselves, their personality, coaches, doctors, psychologists, and the team and life situations. Therefore, the player who has become a professional is more than the sum of the parts that intervened in their process.

This holistic view analyses situations from the multiple interactions that characterise it; that is to say, holism supposes that the performance of a player cannot be determined or explained from one of its parts (for example, only from the physical conditional work), nor by the sum of its components (this conditional work plus training in mental skills, plus technical work, etc.), but the whole system must be considered. In this case, the player behaves in a different way than the sum of all its parts. In other words, the player will generate something different and more important in this situation compared to what each part contributes: their performance and their learning or development depend on where we focus them.

How do you get the coach to think and act from this holistic approach? To begin with, **the coach must**

see people, not players. The person is much more than a player and this implies a major paradigm shift. The person is the great value and the player's person is the one who is going to make decisions, overcome adversities, feel frustrations and sometimes we want to face these moments only from the player's role. We usually hear: *"If you want to be a good player you have to show strength", "You are important for the team, we depend on you", "In football the player who doubts cannot reach excellence"*. However, it is the person under the player's jersey who will support all of these demands.

During all these years, my view of my role as a psychologist was evolving and at that time I saw myself more as someone who generates learning contexts or at least was more aware of them. This holistic perspective is not just another instrument in the toolbox, it is a way of seeing, feeling, breathing and interacting. It has to do with our way of looking at the world and that implies that must be integrated into our being as a psychologists and how we educated our gaze. It cannot be one day holistic and another not, because many times in the work of sports psychologists, as well as coaches, we find several filters that distance us from this holistic perspective, such as the immediacy or the needs of results for team or the player I work with.

I understood at that time that my role in all this is not only to give knowledge or add more to what the coaches or footballers have, but quite the opposite, I had to participate in what was there and purify it. This involved cleaning up the concepts and clarifying them so that they could reach their original meaning. For example, before we spoke of democratic, transformative leadership, and today we can read other distinctions such as conscious, transpersonal leadership. Thus, we are adding meanings to these concepts and at the same time we are moving them away from their essence. In the same breath we find ourselves with the reductionism of the meanings of things, concepts as great as autonomy are for example reduced by not giving the player the solutions of the game.

By this time, new coaches had joined Lezama that were new and younger than before. The meaning of learning had to be revisited and to do this, the meaning of learning needed to be further elaborated.

My initial gaze of learning had evolved into a learning where the focus was no longer just on learning to understand the game, but on learning to push your boundaries, and teaching you to learn something about yourself. I realised that this learning was a crucial task if one wanted to evolve and improve in practice. If we did not evolve in understanding and deepening the concepts we work on, in this case learning, it was going to be difficult to advance in our actions and decisions. This had a lot to do with broadening and deepening the coach's gaze towards learning and, above all, understanding it through how the coach actually lives it within themselves. However this takes time.

We asked ourselves **what questions needed to be asked** in order to review our actions in relation to the internalisation of the players' learning. They had to do with: Where am I as a coach in my learning? What is learning? After all these years, we were not looking for definitions of concepts but rather to understand what is within the concept; for example, what is there in learning? Interaction, reflection, looking at oneself, purposes? Once a week we met to discuss all of these concepts.

In one of the games someone asked, **"What's my purpose as a coach?"** The answers were diverse amongst the coaches: *"To make players for the first team"*, *"That the player arrives at our first team the best they can be as a player and as a person"*. For me in such moments as these the right thing to do is use the silence of reflection that everyone has before giving a reply. It's not an easy question if we haven't thought about it, because when we talk about purpose, we're talking about something both obvious and subtle. Many people recognise what is evident about purpose: they help us move to achieve something. However, that movement and the inner discipline that goes with it has subtle implications. *Which of these two purposes connects you more with your philosophy of life, values, etc.?* In situation I told the coaches, that it may seem like they are the same purpose, but because of those subtleties the purposes are going to be completely different.

I would like to differentiate between the purposes and the objectives. The latter are something more tangible. For example, an objective might be to get two players on to the first team each year. Meanwhile, purposes are something intangible and in my opinion something more vital, in that they connect us to our life and connect us to ourselves; otherwise, we would be talking about sterile purposes, from which nothing flowers. This is key if we want productive and generating people and organisations. The purpose has to do with the purity of my intentions as a coach.

Getting back to the player, the training the player will receive from their coaches will be subtly different. The exercises, the methodology or the physical preparation will be the same; this is the obvious, what is seen and what we can all see, but what is not seen? What are we watching out for? What about the subtle? The subtle is that which is but I do not know, which influences and transforms, but is not seen; it is the hidden, which gives a different touch to the product, this we can call *the coach's touch*. Therefore, it has to be connected to you as a person and it has to do with the coach's ability to gaze and see beyond. In my opinion, all purposes belong in the world of the subtle.

In the social network we live in today, we have created models, fashions, programmes, advice and quick-fix solutions that disconnect us from the sense of what we do and what we want to do. However, my experience tells me that purposes cost a lot to carry out. We usually start them strong and they fade quickly. Sometimes, at the beginning of the projects we propose many things; however, quite a few of them are not carried out. To speak of intention and purpose is something of greater significance. Many times we have our eyes on the goal, on the expectations, on winning in any way and this takes us out of the present moment. Here the purpose calls for putting all the meat on the spit. The purpose is not in grand declarations of intent and it is not in words, it's in day-to-day practice. The coach and all of us have to learn to find these everyday scenarios.

The generosity of intention has to do with the degree of commitment to our daily work. This degree of commitment is a sign of the maturity in people, because it is a choice. The coach is choosing a pure purpose, with no interests or conditions. Choosing is an act of freedom. Opening up this search for a purpose requires us to be very clear about it; you cannot have one foot on one platform and one on the other.

There are no half-measures when it comes to player development, we must have both feet on the same side at all times.

However, what seems so theoretical at first has its development in practice. This choice belongs to another type of contract and different from the one we sign when we start working in an organisation. It belongs to the implicit contract, which has more to do with my willingness to change, to look at the world in a different way than I have done so far and it has to do with my work philosophy. These are the issues that will guide our actions and decisions. Each club should be clear about which implied contract they are asking the coach to live by.

The interiorisation of what we learn has more to do with what we do in our day-to-day life with the player than with what we say. In other words, there has to be consistency between my explicit contract with the project and my implicit contract, which is not said verbally, but is expressed in the actions and decisions we take around the player.

BET ON THE UNDERSTANDING PARADIGM

If we talk about improving the processes of interiorisation of the player, we are talking about understanding. It does not have so much to do with accumulating or giving information as with expanding the player's awareness, i.e. that they realise what they are doing; how are they living it. However, because I don't always realise what's happening to me, we felt that bringing those blind spots out into the open through questioning and conversations was and still is a crucial part of that internalisation.

Talking about internalising was allowing us to look at our interactions with the players and new questions were arising: Do all interactions involve learning? Do all make the player internalise? Whether these interactions produce internalisation will depend on two aspects: the first has to do with where the coach interacts with the player. That is why it was so important for us to look at our intentions when interacting with the player; the second had to do with the coach's ability to generate reflection in the player, that is, the ability to manage the conversation.

After these reflections during the first meetings at this time, we worked on some of the following questions: *How do we understand learning in Lezama? Where am I in my training learning as a coach?*

Several distinctions emerged in the dialogue that we felt were important in understanding how we generate learning in each other and in myself. Some of the coaches' responses were these:

- "I approach learning from how I am learning now, from how I am changing in my way of learning, how I learned before and how I learn now."

- "I ask myself at what point I am ready and able to learn, and why it is important to be curious, receptive and confident. Without losing the mentality of a beginner, in which I start from not knowing and wanting to learn."

- "Since my experience, since the discomfort when I have had situations that have been more difficult for me. Maybe not at the time, but in the process they have allowed me to improve by looking at what I have been doing and how I was doing it or living it. But, when I have felt calmer and more comfortable, believing that I already know this, these situations have not been nutritious for my learning, and not only related to football but a little bit in general. It's important that there is a challenge, a cost or something you have to let go of so that the new can come."

- "Above all it makes me doubt and in that doubt a crack opens up in which I try to give space where different things come in. I'm not able to label it if it's going to be good or bad, it's going to be something different and that I'm going to be something different and for me that's motivating."

From these conversations, this question arose: **What do I have to improve as a coach?** We took the opportunity to focus on it, as I thought it might help to understand how we internalised. The coaches were commenting:

- *"I feel that I don't reach the players; when I talk to them, I feel that my messages doesn't get through. Possibly, it has to do with my current state of confusion, with my need to get it right. My stiffness feels like a self-defence shield. But what am I defending myself against? I understand what it is to do it wrong; especially in the before and during. In the before, I have all the noise that I am not arriving or connecting in this moment, this is a part and it is a detail that that is missing."*
- *"In my training, I miss someone to accompany the coach on the field, to help you see something that you are not seeing of yourself, and at the level of play, not just in learning."*
- *"I personally, when I get here to Lezama, I realise there's a lot I don't know. It is a feeling intertwined with improve through me, and improve through the player and the other person."*

These dialogues were giving me good feedback because I could see what the coach had internalised or not during these years. It was nice because there was a parallel process going on: the coach felt the need to see what the player was or wasn't internalising and I was seeing what the coach had or hadn't internalised.

The following week we opened the dialogue with another question: **How do we learn? How do I know the other person is learning?**

- *"After the experience I had today, from listening to the player's answers and questions and seeing what was coming up, I saw it as information for me; then, being able to see myself, I realised that this information was more about me, about what I don't notice, about what I find hard to accept … and maybe about my limitations too."*

- *"The last day, I was surprised by a player who explained how they learned when they were on the bench … they were viewing another player in their position, seeing themselves reflected in this other player and connecting themselves with the other player's around them … they saw that they were able to distinguish when learning was actually taking place in themselves and the player they were watching."*

- *"I've been thinking about how to get the player to internalise, to take it in. We repeat, I repeat and repeat myself, and I doubt my ability to transmit this internalisation because there is words, there is language, there is communication, but in the end I feel that the player does it because they are told to, not because they feel it is better this way."*

- *One coach ended the day with this question: "I'm talking about the coach too, when they tell us something they want us to internalise, does it reach us, or does it have to do with my receipt of the message? Sometimes we are so full of our own baggage, knowledge or experience that nothing else fits."*

We had already asked these questions in Lezama almost ten years ago, but I understood that the new generations of coaches needed to ask them too. However, I was struck by the responses, they were now more elaborate, more in line with what we had been working on, so some internalisation had been achieved, but above all there was already a certain learning culture in the organisation.

Weeks were passing by and the meetings were moving towards a rethinking of **what we look for in the player**. This would also guide the pedagogy of learning that was being used in Lezama. The answers pointed to issues such as: we want to build autonomy in the player, preparation for the future, knowledge of the game and that they are a conscious player.

This led to one coach concluding, ***"How to convert or transform the passive subject into an active subject?*** *With reflection, self-criticism, habits of dialogue, preparing to train, encouraging the player to be responsible for their learning. This is what takes up most of my time"..*

The situation opened up new questions for us:

• What about all the things I can learn that is not visible, because we need to see answers (performance)?

- Are there hidden learnings?
- How does a player learn to be afraid of the ball? Only when you show it?
- Maybe you've learned it before?

The players were also aware of their training process, of the differences they found in Lezama's coaches. These are some of the answers to surveys that were made to players about the learning model:

After this reflection on the pedagogy of learning, a diagnosis was made of the needs of each category, of the needs of the player according to their age and the skills that the coach needed to face these evolutionary moments of the player.

We started from a brief article that I was given to by its author Pep Mari, at the CAR in San Cugat[23] many years ago, in which a pyramid appeared that caught my attention and that over time we evolved it.

---

23   Head of the Sports Psychology Department at the High Performance Sports Centre in Sant Cugat (Barcelona).

María Ruiz De Oña

What does the player need to learn for them to be a competitive professional player?

COMPETITIVE PLAYER

TO KNOW HOW TO COMPETE.

SELF-CONSCIOUS

We want teams, player's with a **consistent performance**, that is also controlled. To manage their emotions, psychological variables and to cope with the adversities from the competition.

LEARNING TO LEARN. AUTONOMY

A THINKING PLAYER with GOALS, FEEDBACK, 1ST PERSON SPEAKING, TAKING DECISIONS. Sometimes players don't accept their mistakes, "*the fault is that of the others*", then what does this player learn? **Players need to understand why and what they are doing the task or the football exercise for?**

DESIRE TO LEARN. COMMITMENT

Our motivation for learning, for changing, to come out of our comfort zone... When we want to achieve something good, it is never for free, you have to pay the price. **Are you willing to pay that price to be a better coach?**

ABILITY TO LEARN. DISCIPLINE

On the one hand our OPERATING STYLE (personality) doesn't allow us to learn, for instance; perfectionism, pessimism, fears... and sometimes our old experiences, past learning, our beliefs or all of them, create resistance in ourselves to learn and to change. We need healthy inner habits to think. On the other hand we have to have healthy external HABITS & BEHAVIOURS: DISCIPLINE and HEALTHY FAMILY ENVIRONMENT.

To be able to learn. Sometimes our style of operation does not help us to learn. For example, perfectionism, a tendency to pessimism, fears. Other times, old experiences, past learnings, beliefs or loyalties are what can create resistance or limitations to learning. All learning involves some change and all change involves a loss.

Wanting to learn. It refers to the motivation to learn, to change, to get out of our comfort zone. When we want to achieve something good, it's never for free, you have to pay a price. Are you willing to pay that price to be a better player or coach?

Knowing how to learn. To create learning environments where the player can learn to learn, where they speak in first person (to me, my difficulty, about me (oneself)), where they are asked and asks questioning questions that take them to an unknown territory, it must be challenging for them, while also being able to ask and give feedback and not falling into excuses. It is hard to take advantage of a training session if I don't know, before starting it, what objectives I must achieve and how I must work to achieve them. We have to look for the cause of our mistakes in ourselves. If you don't admit you've done something wrong, you won't stop to analyse it. You won't find anything to rectify and you won't change anything, so you'll probably repeat the same mistake over and over again. For example, I will hardly make progress if when I fail,

I waste an opportunity to improve, and continue to attribute this mistake on the field.

Knowing how to compete. Learning to have consistency, regularity in performance, through understanding the emotions that arise in me when I compete. Learning to face the adversities that competition presents to me.

From the perspective of this pyramid, the stages of each category and player age in the Lezama cantera was analysed, from which the following pathway of needs emerged. For your understanding, while the name of each category is in Spanish, it is defined in English with regards to the age of the players within the specific category and typically how many years these players have been in the Lezama cantera (Athletic Bilbao Club Football Academy). Furthermore, there is also a section at the end of this book titled *'Football Categories in Spain and Athletic Club Bilbao'* that will give you more guidance on these categories pathways.

LEARNING NEEDS FOR ATHLETIC BILBAO CLUB - GROUP & CATEGORIES

ALEVÍN (10 YEAR OLD PLAYERS; 1ST YEAR IN THE LEZAMA CANTERA)

- **Landing in Lezama**: The discipline in everyday life, from learning how to organise and take responsibility for the training material or the importance of timing, including internalising the intensity of training and understanding Lezama's own football concepts.

- Understanding **the need for having order** in the functioning of the Lezama cantera and learning habits: participating in the dressing room; reflecting in first person. Having respect for the coaches, fellow teammates, punctuality, the supplied material and post-shower and recover time after training sessions and games.

- **Working on individual and shared responsibility**. Players need to internalise and to realise that all their actions have reciprocity for them and for the group through the natural consequences that their decisions and actions generate. Through dialogue, it is an important moment to bring out those natural consequences that are often there but not seen and make them conscious in the player to learn them.

- **New learning culture**. The player usually comes from a short-sighted culture of results. The player comes from another way of understanding the competition, meaning they are focused on Sunday's game rather than on learning. It is important to initiate the player into a culture focused on a learning process in which the result will be a consequence of them.

- These players can come with a passive attitude to learning, i.e. waiting to be told what to do and how. We need to initiate them into an **active-thinking player attitude**, i.e. the player participates in their learning through their own reflection, dialogue and reflection with the coach and other players.

- **To initiate them in Dialogical Learning**: To habituate them to think and to speak in first person. To create an awareness of learning. At this stage they can all speak at once, so they have to learn to take turns with respect and also need to understand the importance of working in silence.

ALEVÍN-INFANTIL (11-12 YEAR OLD PLAYERS; 2ND AND 3RD YEAR IN THE LEZAMA CANTERA)

- **Difficulties**. One experience that this group finds is the difficulty of the opponent in the competition and the implications that this entails depending on how the player perceives it: as a challenge or as a threat. Fears appear, i.e. they are many losses; not always playing in Lezama; worried about what other people say; the influence of the scoreboard. There is also a resistance to change and an intolerance towards frustration. In players and coaches it is important to build a capacity to understand these frustrations.

- They need to understand the importance of training and that the competition is also a learning context.

- Work on the understanding and meanings of why this difficulty is sought (in competition; in our fears), what it is to win and lose? What is to compete?

- Deepen the objectives with respect to the scoreboard. Deepen the subject, i.e. the principles of the game.

INFANTIL 2º AÑO (13 YEAR OLD PLAYERS; 4ᵀᴴ YEAR IN THE LEZAMA CANTERA)

- **The work on learning objectives** is important again. Targets need to be above the competition. The difficulty of the competition is low in this league and therefore is minimum challenge with the competition being easy.

- Friendly tournaments are the mirror of the team's progress in this group.

- Attention to the perception of reality. Educating in self-demanding and nonconformity is important.

• This is the year with the most casualties from the Lezama cantera, meaning it's the year with the highest number of players coming and going.

CADETE 1º AÑO (14 YEAR OLD PLAYERS; 5ᵀᴴ YEAR IN THE LEZAMA CANTERA)

• **Reinforce internal discipline.** This includes habits, commitments, functional order and responsibility. To understand that what I decide as a player has a consequence on me that either favours or impairs me.

• Resistances appear in their Learning. Beliefs like *"I'm good"*, *"He always tells me"* or *"I'm going to the national team"* and adolescence are small barriers that the coach needs to manage. However, on the other hand, the player must interiorise the objectives, the questions, and the dialogue in the dressing room, including speaking in first person and that entails a greater capacity of self-questioning of the player, therefore greater critical reflection. An example of this greater critical reflection was when one coach expressed, *"They feel more autonomous, they don't buy everything you tell them anymore"*.

• There is a greater demand for the game and a need to deepen it. This demand of the game will expose the player, it will show them their weaknesses and whether or not they can take another step. The player realises this within themselves: *"Some people make progress and I don't, even though I try my best,"* said one player. That's why these resistors appear, to protect them. In this category, details in training become more important.

• Another issue that players need to understand is why and for what purpose are the different age stages shared. Why do we train in groups with those who are a year younger or a year older than me?

• They have to face more difficult tournaments and this sometimes means losing all the games. What function do these tournaments have for them? What do they involve?

CADETE 2º AÑO (15 YEAR OLD PLAYERS, 6ᵀᴴ YEAR IN THE LEZAMA CANTERA)

• At this age, many of these players will have been working with this learning philosophy for five years now in Lezama.

• The day-to-day working style in responsibility, autonomy, philosophy, training method and active participation in their learning are already internalised if everything has gone their way.

• The player feels more absent in their development, they are stalling, and their energy is coming and going while all the time feeling inconsistent in their being. Their level of maturity allows for debate and questioning. They can already elaborate messages with arguments.

- There may be a decline in their participation in collective learning and a setback in commitment towards preparing for training sessions and competitions.

- The allocation of minutes is beginning to be more selective.

- They win almost every game and that means undemanding and unchallenging competition. How do we coaches compensate for this? The demand on training and on your individual needs is vital at this stage. This offers another mirror for player to look inside themselves in order to avoid constructing misconceptions of oneself.

Once the needs of the players in the different stages of their learning in Lezama have been defined, we start to define the resources that they must master in order to develop. Furthermore, it follows the same pyramid structure that we referred to before.

RESOURCES FOR LEARNING TO LEARN ACCORDING TO THE CATEGORY

ALEVÍN (10 YEAR OLD PLAYERS, 1ST YEAR IN THE LEZAMA CANTERA)

- Introduce them to the **principles of the game**, to speaking in **first person** and working with the **objectives** that are focused on the principles of the game and finally learning how to use them.

- New players are very competition-oriented. The coach needs to be very internalised and understand **the importance of training**. Training is the most important thing, because many times the competition doesn't offer us as many opportunities to solve for the player. The coach needs to be aware of the weight they place on the training and the competition through their attitude, behaviour and words, so that the importance of commitment to training becomes apparent to the player.

- At the same time, it is important for the coach in this category to feel that **the competition is a means** and to believe in it.

- The player needs to learn to think. They need to get used to interacting, participating and thinking about their internal feedback, difficulties and solutions to the game, and how they relate to all of this.

ALEVÍN–INFANTIL (11-12 YEAR OLD PLAYERS, 2ND & 3RD YEAR IN THE LEZAMA CANTERA)

- Learning to **listen**. Respecting the rhythm of the conversation. Begin to realise that in the **silences** you also learn. The players' are encouraged to talk without the need to raise their hand.
- These players get used to interacting, participating and thinking about their internal feedback, difficulties and solutions to the game, and how they relates to all this.
- Introduce the players to each other's **feedback**.
- Deepening in the meanings of winning/losing and success. Becoming aware of the influence of the defending player. Facing the transition from 7-aside football to 11-aside and dealing with excuses like: *"in 7-aside football it was different..."*

INFANTIL–CADETE (13/14/15 YEAR OLD PLAYERS, 4TH 6TH YEAR IN LEZAMA CANTERA)

- These are typically great years to go deeper into individual goals, because the rivals doesn't give you much of a challenge. It is important to work on knowing how to detect if I am in the **comfort zone** and learn how to get out of it through nonconformity.
- The player needs to be aware and to question whether they are **committing** themselves to their improvement.

- To initiate the player into the fact that all people have a **blind spot**, that is something I do not see about myself, but the others do. These blind spots need to be looked at and accepted so they can be improved.

- Manage the dialogues as a tool for self-knowledge, by also deepening the game with what we do and how we do it.

María Ruiz De Oña

What do players need to learn to be competitive professional players?

COMPETITIVE PLAYER

TO KNOW HOW TO COMPETE

EMOTIONS

To be consistent

LEARNING TO LEARN

LEARNING CONTEXT IN THE TRAINING SESSION & COMPETITION

Speaking in First Person/objectives/feedback/out of comfort Zone/dealing with mistakes/accepting criticism.

DESIRE TO LEARN

COMMITMENT & RESPONSIBILITY

Consequences /Excuses/Prepare myself to cope with the adversities /Demanding/Effort

ABILITY TO LEARN

FAMILY ENVIRONMENT

DISCIPLINE/HABITS: Timetables/attitude to cope with adversities/rules

OPERATING STYLE: TRENDS OF BEING/BEHAVING: hard-worker, lazy, responsible/perfectionism, pessimism, good/ low awareness about myself, self-criticism

REFLECTION ABOUT PSYCHOLOGICAL AND LEARNING NEEDS OF PLAYERS IN ACCORDANCE TO THEIR AGE

Once the players' needs had been analysed, in the same vein, we had to attend to the work of the coaches in this same process, for which it is necessary to define the skills needed by the coaches at each category stage. This means to also understand the shadows and blind spots they have to encounter in their own work.

COACHING SKILLS NEEDED

It is a question of defining what skills, also understood as knowledge, which the coach's need to respond to the needs of the players and what shadows and blind spots are in their work.

ALEVÍN (10 YEAR OLD PLAYERS, 1ST YEAR IN THE LEZAMA CANTERA)

• The coach needs to be able to **synthesise the principles of the game** and handle the nomenclature by adapting to the child's lexicon.

• **Be clear and understand that everything starts from the knowledge of the game**. The first player stage at 10 years old is at the origin of the training process and so the player must be initiated into the principles of the game.

•   *The coach's shadows:* This can be putting players in positions without thinking about the player's improvement. Sometimes, the coach changes the player's position because of the needs of the game or the opponent, rather than thinking about the needs of the player. The coach can instrumentalise the player for their benefit.

• The coach has to **talk to the player about playing the game, not scoring**. The coach needs to understand the implications of the view of competition as a means of learning. It's something we need to be aware of.

  • *Coach's shadows:* They appear when the coach feels the fear of losing both in league games and in tournaments.

• **The player is the value**. When is this value in danger? In a contexts where competition may make the coach stop the development of the cadet stages (14-15 year old players) moving forward. In higher categories, the culture of short-termism creates more pressure for the coaches. Perhaps external factors such as agents, parents and fans also have an influence. Where does the coach have to be clear about this? With the youngest players.

  • *The coach's shadows*: This happens when we think of our interests only and are invaded by our insecurities

• **The player plays in the position that makes them grow**. In the alevín category (10 year old players), it is key that players are changed to positions based on their improvement. For example, if the player is a good runner, you put them on the inside; if there not aggressive in duels, they need to have experiences in defence, even if they are not going to be a defender. If they are good playing in midfield then playing in the hallway/through the middle is their improvement position. It is vital that all players especially during the early years in the Lezama cantera have two positions; a future position and a position of improvement.

- The coach needs to **understand why training is the most important thing** and needs to convey this to the player. It's necessary for the player to see when they enter Lezama that training is central to their entire development process as a player. This is what will give them control of their progression and learning.

- ***The coach's shadows:*** when the coach is outperforming the competition, they need to ***have*** everything under control. This means training puts you at the service of the competition.

- **Getting started in Learning**. Part of the need for the player's, is active participation in their learning. For this, the interaction between the coach and player is important. The question for the coach is; *not what do I have to teach and how will I do it? But what does the player have to learn, how will they learn it and how will they show the coach that they have learned?*

- **Be available**, work on the observations and the listening in order to get to know the player and to be able to reach them.
- The coach must be clear and conscious about what details are not to be passed on to the player. The coach and player need to be **more demanding in the type of detail**, so for example with the youngest players, the coaches can't escape the details of the game and need to avoid players growing up with excuses.

ALEVÍN-INFANTIL (11-12 YEAR OLD PLAYERS; 2ND AND 3RD YEAR IN THE LEZAMA CANTERA)

- Transfer from 7 aside Football to 11 aside Football. The coach needs to understand where the player is coming from.
- The coach needs to understand that the scoring result is not the indicator of the player's progress. The coach needs to learn to **evaluate the qualitative indicators of the player's progress** in all its facets: in the game, in their learning and in their maturing process.
- The coach needs to have internalised **the place of the result** and its management. It cannot be affected by the result. It must be managed from the knowledge of the game. This is the knowledge from where we are able to face the difficulties of the competition in terms of the fact that the rivals are physically older.

We understand that the coach has to be internalised in all of these development factors.

- Beware of instrumentalising the player; that is seeing the player as an object that is serving the interests of others.

- The trainer needs to understand what implications their decisions have towards both training preparation and planning. The focus is on **working from what the player needs to progress**. We strongly accentuated this foundation in the players for the infantile 2º año stage (13 years old), because it had the least challenging competition, and also in the players for the cadet 1º año stage (14 years old), because it was felt that is where the most casualties were happening with players coming and going each year. The player needs to be aware of their importance.

> - **The coach's shadows**: when decisions are made thinking about the score, the opponent, the team, and not about what is best for the player's improvement.

- It's important that I expose the player and that I don't protect them. The player plays in the position that makes them grow.

> - **The coach's shadows**: when the coach makes decisions to the detriment of the player's needs only to strengthen the team, to feel more confident, etc.

- **More demanding in the details**. During this year, the competition will allow the coach to look at the details so that the player does not conform. If your opponent outperforms you, it's harder to focus on the details.

- The coach needs to be aware of **how their conversations with the players are going**, they need to reflect on whether the spaces for the interaction between the player-coach on the field, changing room, etc., are characterised by the educational contexts and go deeper into them. How much space do I leave for the player to talk or think? How much space do I take up as a coach? The coach must be aware of their ability to listen, to grasp what is not being said, what the player does not count as being important or what they don't see, more so, what is the reason behind it. The coach needs to be introduced to **the use of the questioning question**. This is the one that more than answers but gives me knowledge of myself in a situation.

INFANTIL-CADETE 1º AÑO (13-14 YEARS OLD, 4TH AND 5TH YEAR IN THE LEZAMA CANTERA)

- Rigor, firmness in philosophy (in decisions about the player) and investing in a culture of learning with the player. To take care not to lose focus on why and what we are here for.

- Mastering the application of the philosophy towards the tournaments. Knowing how to read the performance in the tournaments. They are a reference to the player's progress.

- Knowing how to see and understand the learning rates of the player. Knowing how to manage discipline from understanding and relationship.

- Knowing how to look further about what you're seeing.

- The coach needs to have already internalised how to put into action the philosophy by which, **through the improvement of the player, they improve the team**. We put it in at this stage because it is the moment of change from the low exigency of the infantile category (12-13 year old players) to a high exigency in the cadet category (14-15 year old players). Improvement at an individual level is key; for example, duels, not only in the physical aspect but also in attitude and execution, since in the infantile players, they do it unintentionally and in cadets it is no longer valid.

- *The coach's shadows:* hiding in the team (general, open, team-centred messages).

- **Long-term vision of the player**. It's the coach's ability to project the player into the future.

- *The coach's shadow:* when the results put pressure on you as a coach it can make you feel like a failure straightaway. Therefore, I decide, I do and I resolve; that is to say, it falls into the need to win above anything else, without taking into account that the one who has to win in this situation is the player with their learning.

• **Individual improvement within collective work**. In this case, the coach's shadow would be in stages where the result hides the difficulties of the player's progress.

CADETE 2º AÑO (15 YEAR OLD PLAYERS, 6TH YEAR IN THE LEZAMA CANTERA)

• **Challenge the player**. Insist that the player needs to outdo themselves. There is no competitive difficulty with minimum challenges from games and tournaments in this category. In this moment, it's all part of us and each other. The fact that there are no competing demands can lead to mistakes.

• The environment and the results are beginning to take hold and make a repercussion influence. The player becomes more selfish: being a starter; if they don't play, they complain or get angry. Comparisons are given between players, between parents and representatives appear. What the outside world will say appears at this stage and there are players who feel a lot of pressure.

• **Training is the most important thing**. The wear and tear that comes with conveying the training philosophy which is the important thing, leads to more collisions and confrontations with the player.

- It's easy to fall for the self-deception. To think that the score is indicative of the dominance of the game.

- **Care for details**. Importance of taking care of details by the coach.

LEARNING ENVIROMENT

P L A Y E R

UNDERSTANDING COMPETITION
* It is the manifestation of what has been learned
* It is a mirror of the coach's job
* It is the control of the work from the week

CONSISTENCY OF PERFORMANCE
* Prepare for competition
* Capability to overcome themselves
* Presence and take decisions under pressure
* Determination: attitude to go for it
* Face adversities of competition
* Recovers quickly from setback

TO CREATE A LEARNING CULTURE
* To challenge
* Questions
* Responsible (First person speaking)
* Feedback

TO LEARN TO THINK
* To talk in First Person
* To come out of their comfort zone
* To give and ask for feedback
* Setting goals

MENTOR SELF-AWARENESS
* To explore and focus the player
* To listen
* To see beyond
* To connect with the player

TO BE CONSCIOUS
* What limits and empowers my learning?
* To comprehend (to give meaning to what I do) & to understand myself

SELF-KNOWLEDGE PHILOSOPHY

SELF-DISCIPLINE SELF-OBSERVE

Coach

María Ruiz De Oña

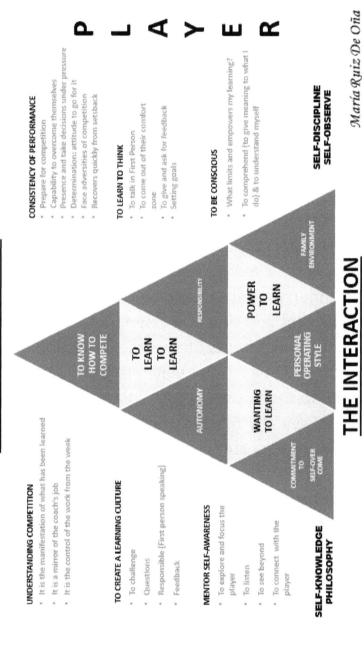

TO KNOW HOW TO COMPETE

TO LEARN TO LEARN

RESPONSIBILITY

POWER TO LEARN

FAMILY ENVIRONMENT

AUTONOMY

WANTING TO LEARN

PERSONAL OPERATING STYLE

COMMITMENT TO SELF-OVER COME

THE INTERACTION

During this time, the pyramid was getting more content with consistency. In addition, we integrated, parallel to the learning process of the player, those elements that the coaches had found along the way in their learning.

These reflections on how we could get the player to internalise what they are learning and to make the learning more sustainable over time, led us to review the needs of the categories, groups and players in the Lezama cantera. More importantly, what was all of this asking of us as coaches?

We understood that learning follows a retrogressive movement and that it is essential to know how to detect those moments of impasse, recession and advancements in which the player is living. Many times we jump to conclusions when a player seems to stop, does not give any more or when the performance is not what we expected.

There were still questions to reflect on, questions that had been opened up to us and questions that led us to continue to ask ourselves, what we are doing? And how we are doing it? This vital learning that we are talking about and the learning that I believe Lezama is nourished by is endless. It is this infinite horizon that we consider proper education that keeps it alive and keeps our *gaze* alive.

These last few years were a time of high turnover of coaches; virtually all of the veteran coaches who had been part of building this process had left the Athletic Bilbao Club Academy. However, the learning culture was already immersed in the day-to-day life in Leza-ma, with more or less quality. However, you could breathe and sense it in both the young coaches and the others who were more reticent about the project.

CHAPTER 9
STARTING OVER

As I pointed out in the first pages of this book, it is necessary to understand the formation process of a competitive player with all its complexity. Things are no longer jack, horse and king; that is, something pre-established that is repeated in time. **To simplify that complexity is to reduce the person and therefore to limit them.**

I am clear that the football exercises, all the planning or the technologies are not the ones that develop the human being by themselves, it is through the spaces of interaction that are given between the player and the coach. This is the place where the learning is situated and where it emerges. These spaces are the axis of this proposal and are characterised by being educational contexts; that is, contexts where people's potential is developed.

If we review the type of actions that we put into play in these interactions, we will see that many of them are not only related to the technical competence but also to the personal competence. Therefore, coaches need to develop actions and conversations with players that affect both the sports environment and the personal.

This space of interaction is built through a relationship horizontality, from person to person (subject-subject). The relationship between the coach and player is one of learning where both learn. Only when the coach realises that place and space, does the player's vital learning flow.

But let's look at what has been in these interactions so that they have a learning value.

• To have and embody a **philosophy of work** as a coach. Understanding this work as beliefs or principles that serve the coach as a guide for their decisions and actions in a way that helps them to face different situations in their daily life.

• **To be present, open and available** to whatever may be emerging in the conversation with the player. This means having no judgment.

• **A systemic view**. It is an integrative, not exclusive view that puts the focus on both the interactions and on the gaze at what is seen and what is not seen in the collective.

• **He listens to her. Listen to yourself and listen to the other person**. When I listen, I have to be aware that I am starting a journey with the other person and I have to let myself go. The one who listens does so by going light of baggage: only to be present and available to the other. Judgments, hypotheses, quick advice and arguments have no place in this backpack on this journey. The key is to understand the message through listening to what is said and what is not said, to listen to the emotion that is hidden or shown and, above all, from what inner place of the person it is generated. Doing so will help me give a meaning and build a common space of expression. By using the silence, paraphrasing, and returning the last words of the sentence that the player is saying to me, will make them see that I am listening to them. Additionally, reflecting what the other is saying to me with their words, helps in this moment of listening. Interpretations, advice, encouragement, agreements, disagreements, sermons or corrections will have to wait for their time to appear if necessary.

> *"It's important to ask myself, how what the other person is saying impacts on me as a coach or psychologist," in the words of Javier Garcia de Andoin.*

- **First-person learning**. This must be the first way of learning, since we refer to everything that happens to oneself by answering these questions: Where am I? What's happening to me? How do I relate to what's happening to me?

- The place where the conversation takes place. It must be in the player's **unknown territory**, in their shadows or blind spots, because it is these parts that need light to grow.

- **The question**. We build interaction through questions. However, not all questions open up questioning spaces in the player. The questioning question is one that gives me knowledge of myself in a situation, not just answers. This is the question that generates true knowledge. Therefore, a series of guidelines should be followed to take you on a pathway in this very important direction:

  - First, I need to be able to question myself.

  - A good question is born from good listening.

  - Be clear about the purpose of the question: Why do I ask this question?

  - The questions do not question the person, only the ideas and beliefs that they question. We must move forward with sharp and precise questions that are at the same time loving and understanding.

- **The silence** generated by a question is a good sign of the value of the question. "Silence is what sustains everything". [24]

- **The feedback**. We learn with the other person, because the other makes us the mirror. We know

---

24   Javier Garcia de Andoin in one of the workshops we did with Self Institute.

that without the other person, it is very hard to learn. In the working groups with the coaches and the players, we have to introduce the need to be aware of my blind spots, meaning everything I don't see about myself.

- **Security floor**. This is the unconditional love that a coach must give to a player regardless of their performance and the results. It is the recognition of the player as a valid, capable person, regardless of whether or not they achieve their objectives. What happens when the love we receive is conditioned by our achievements?

- **The dialogue**. This is understood as a means of self-knowledge. Dialogue raises questions, interrogates and takes us beyond our comfort zone. A dialog can be opened from:

    - **The coach** who makes a small introduction of a topic i.e., something that happened during the week, something that happened between the group, about aspects of the game, emotions that have arisen, etc.

    - From **the player**: The coach asks the group, does anyone have anything to bring to this conversation? Anyone want to bring up a subject or a certain point of view? And it is the player who initiates the dialogue with another question to the group or by exposing some doubts or concerns.

"Often the dialogue has to incorporate the shadows of the group itself, meaning what is hidden and what is unknown within the group. The dialogue gives voice to the player's hidden agendas, insights or emerging intuitions into the learning of the dialogue itself. This is something that the coach, psychologist, etc, will have to intuit or observe and put it out into the open".[25]

- **Working on the beliefs and emotions**. With the particularity that many times these beliefs and emotions are hidden, so it is important that the coach learns to listen to what the player says and what they do not say.

From my experience, the traditional model of work, based on *me teaching you and you learning*, has fallen from any discipline such as Psychology. We know what kind of player it leads to, but for many it is and has been the way to work. Changing the concept of working, training and seeing the development of the player means breaking down many beliefs and above all leaving our territory of the known. I am not referring to methodologies, player profiles, structures, planning and pre-established routes, but to a way of viewing the formation of the person within football. A way that allows him/her to develop all his/her po-

---

25   Javier Garcia de Andoin in one of the workshops we did with Self-Institute.

tential and acquire the necessary maturity in terms of autonomy and responsibility to face the future of the game. Finally, all this leads to educating and being educators as well as coaches and psychologists.

This work proposal is humanistic. The human being, the person, the professional is the one who can empower it and the one who can limit it.

My time at Athletic Bilbao Club over two decades gave me a lot of food for thought. In these pages I have tried to gather all these experiences and put them into words, something that I sincerely find very difficult. I can't pigeonhole everything into models or methods because I feel that they kill the dynamism and fluidity of learning. This has been a way of working organically and understanding a gaze (La Mirada) that is alive. I know that what has to evolve will evolve and what has to die will die.

EPILOGUE

I am going to go back in time, a quarter of a century to recall what began to take shape in those days. It was a good time to take a look into the future and to verbalise the uncertainties, with some key questions we had within Athletic Club Bilbao.

- Will we be able to remain competitive?
- Will Lezama be able to meet those needs?
- In what context will we view each other in a few years?

Because of our responsibility to what Athletic Club Bilbao represents and the mission we have together with it, we had to project for a viable future and that horizon of durability should guide us in our way of doing and interacting at all levels.

We needed a new paradigm. A criticism review was not enough and it was necessary to write up, reformulate and plant what reference guides we were going to live by. This meant understanding **the development of the player,** as a value to the project, and doing so through the hand of the **coaches and**

professionals in Lezama, by a formative context of a **common approach.**

In the '96/'97 season we signed an agreement with the University of Deusto in Bilbao and created the Department of Psychology in Lezama with the great objective of collaborating in the development of the player. I remember the moments of the first conversations outlining the first steps to be taken and how to intervene, when we agreed that not only the players, but also the coaches needed support, and that it had to be implemented on this combined pathway.

We were on a trajectory of generating a learning culture and with this perspective, we would give true value to the role of the coach. Time has confirmed this for us.

The formation of people was part of our culture and it became an emerging property to the life in Lezama in which the player was immersed.

A fine rain was beginning to seep around the training methods, giving credence to the idea that at the core of learning lies the key to the progression of youth preparation systems, and that success was not synonymous with winning. It was learning, generating, and gaining knowledge.

The big objective was the evolution of the player, and decisions had to go in that direction. The development of the player was an end in itself, and their learning process was key, giving them the true protagonist to their own path.

María helped us to reinforce this idea as our great objective, and to give it a differentiating character. Just as if we were goldsmiths, putting all ourselves into the player's benefit in order to guarantee the progression of this young person towards their maximum possibilities.

The idea of a common approach was another of the strategic keys. It was fundamental to foster a feeling of belonging and mutual support, and to generate a culture to be modelled with the participation of all. This involved all the passionate professionals within the club, who had concerns and worries, who wanted to learn, and together we would go hand in hand.

I have to confess, gathering reflections from the Dutch philosopher Erasmus of Rotterdam[26], and thinking that this longed for a union of professionals working on the development of the player, under a club statement of a common culture, language and principles. It is still an unexecuted utopia and perhaps never executable within our reality.

This does not mean that it is not exciting and motivating as a vital impulse and, although it is difficult to achieve, it is presented as a maxim and a reference that helps us not to get side tracked by the desires of

_____
26   A Dutch philosopher who embraced the humanistic belief in an individual's capacity for self-improvement and the fundamental role of education.

our egos and short-termism, but rather by ideas in which processes flow based on a philosophy of training, integration and participation.

A project of this magnitude needs to be supported by courageous people, with the capacity to assume responsibilities and fundamentally committed to serving an ideal, based on an integrating commitment and by polluting leadership with the transmitting and creating of value.

I remember with nostalgia those first years, how you María accompanied us, you were part of the project, as an apprentice, as a teacher, and you had an enthusiasm that gave us a lot of strength.

In this transit, the great evolution has been achieved through the training of Lezama's professionals, giving value and competence to many vocational educators, scholars and enthusiasts in this wonderful role has become one of your mottos and principles.

María, in the depths of your gaze, there is a reflection that I highlight, it is the distinction between the objective and the purpose, that core idea, which has guided us on this journey. It is the gaze which synthesises the great direction in which, I defend, is the one which we must conduct our self in within this complex world of the development of people in a football context.

To educate, and to form, it is the same as to put a motor into a boat, these are words of Gabriel Celaya[27], extracted from one of his poems. These words can illustrate and give us the light to improve and to project these and other ideas to others.

We have shared a lot of road together and you point out to us that in these years you have changed your way of gazing, not only yours, but that of many who have shared experiences with you and who have contributed to having a wider and deeper vision. As well as a willingness to change permanently and above all, a willingness to change in oneself, that is a real learning experience.

We are part of an entity that plays an important role in our society, so we have the responsibility to be committed to the formation of people, and increasingly being better prepared to serve as role models to others. It is essential to focus on a formative-educational model that permeates, and one that serves as a vehicle so that both young people and professionals are well integrated and trained in the face of challenges of this nature, which are very broad in outlook and very demanding.

Therefore, the training projects that can be developed in Athletic Club Bilbao, and centralised in its facilities in Lezama, have a special importance, as a response to the needs of the Club throughout its history.

Jose Mari Amorrortu

---

27   A Spanish poet who studied engineering.

THE AUTHORS

María Ruiz de Oña: In the world of football that is full of uncertainty, pressure and the need to adapt to change, it is essential that coaches foster a culture of learning where a challenging environment is created to develop competitive players. María Ruiz de Oña, a psychologist with 21 years of experience at Athletic Club Bilbao, where she was responsible for the Psychology and Learning Education for coaches and players.

This was the beginning of a new learning step for the Club and was in conjunction with her studies and research in Psychology from the University of Deusto. Founding member of AIPAF (International Association of Psychology Applied to Football), currently, María is working in Aspire Academy in Doha, Qatar as the Lead Psychologist for the Football Development & Performance Department. Her main activity in this role is the mentoring-training of the coaches in a project with a philosophy focused on the development of the player while also educating coaches and players on what it is to develop a competitive player in high performance football.

María, promotes vital learning to achieve a harmonious, integral and balanced development of the person and the teams through self-knowledge, listening, understanding the words we use, sensitivity, intuition and promoting the valuable learning gained from educating and understanding the gaze through psychology. Her speciality is in group learning as an agent of change and innovation for football clubs and other organisations.

In more than 20 years of her experience, María has managed to collaborate professionally with some of the following Clubs and Federations: América de México, Bayer Leverkusen, Rubin Kazan, Villareal, New York City, Premier League, Chilean Football Federation, Italian Federation of Football and Zenit of Saint Petersburg. María has also collaborated in the development of professionals from the management world: Global Zurich, Euskaltel, Forum Manager, Expo Coaching, European University of Madrid, Florida University of Valencia and Victory University (Australia) among others. María, understands that many times 'Everybody wants to change everybody, but they don't want to change themselves, and that change must first happen in ourselves'.

John O'Neill: A Sport Psychologist who is from and currently based in Ireland. Since 2015, John has been travelling to Athletic Club Bilbao learning about their Psychology and the Personal Development methods they implement with their coaches and players. That was the first year that John and María started to co-llaborate, learn, and share psychology concepts and projects with each other in elite football. From such learning opportunities, John was able to apply his Psychology MSc Dissertation to Athletic Club Bilbao's unique approach to developing home-grown players within La Liga.

With both María and John having an aligned out-look on development and what this actually means for each person and organisation, it has been a very interesting mentoring relationship in understanding the psychology needed for the development of coa-ches and players in high performance football. This includes having a strong belief with each other in un-derstanding the function of vulnerability within the player, coach, team and club, and how can it be used to promote learning. While also seeing the impor-tance in helping coaches to face their own fears and blind spots before helping the players to do likewise. This is especially important when María's and John's objective of psychology for a club is to develop the potential of the player through the development of the coach.

Over the last number of years, John has been on collaborative learning spaces professionally with some of the following Clubs and Organisations; Arsenal Football Club, Manchester City, Manchester United, Leeds United, Nike Football Academy and FC Bayern Munich. After completing his undergrad degree in Sport & Exercise Science, John completed an MSc in Sport, Exercise & Performance Psychology with both programmes completed at the University of Limerick, Ireland. Currently, John is undertaking a PhD with the Psychology Department at Mary Immaculate College, Ireland where he is investigating what can be achieved when we allow vulnerability to lead and coach us in the learning context of the group as problem-solving on a one-to-one basis may not solve a problem group-wide. This can often be the case in football development when a player gets broken up into different departments and data within a club, meaning there is a chance the player will break. Understanding the vulnerability within these relationships is one of the main pillars of work that María and John collaborate closely on in order to achieve a more concrete and applied framework of research that makes a development impact especially within elite football.

BIBLIOGRAPHICAL REFERENCES

- Andrea Ruffinelli. *Reflective teacher training: a focus on construction and dispute*. March. 2017.
- David Bohm. *About the dialogue*. 1997.
- Essay on *"Pedagogy of Autonomy"* by Paolo Freire Chapter I: *"No Teaching without Discord"*. 2004.
- Giovani Reale and Dario Antiseri. *History of philosophical and scientific thought*. 1988.
- Guillermo Echegaray. *Organisational Constellations*. 2013.
- John Berger. *Ways of seeing. London*. 2008.
- Juan Domingo Farnós. *Innovation and Knowledge*. EduTech Wiki. 2007.
- Juan Domingo Farnós. *Learning theories*. Retrieved February 7, 2009 https://juandomingofarnos. wordpress.com
- Maite Dárceles. *Guide to transformation*. Provincial Council of Bizkaia. 2009
- Marius Bomholt. *Artworks that Look at You (and Themselves) Reflections on the Gaze (La Mirada) in Lacan, Didi-Huberman, and Pfaller*. 2020.

- Mezirow, Jack. *Learning as a transformation critical perspectives on a theory in progress.* 2000.
- Otto Scharmer. *Theory U: Leading from the Future as It Emerges.* 2009.
- Paolo Freire. Pedagogy of autonomy. 1970.

FOOTBALL CATEGORIES
SPAIN & ATHLETIC CLUB BILBAO

TYPICAL FOOTBALL CATEGORIES IN SPAIN

- Benjamín: (8-9 years old)   This age category is not in Athletic Club Bilbao.
- Alevín: (10-11 years old)   In Euskadi (The Basque Country) - 7-aside school
- Infantil: (12-13 years old)   11-aside School Football
- Cadete: (14-15 years old)   Federated Football
- Juvenil: (16-17-18 years old)   Federated Football

FOOTBALL CATEGORIES IN ATHLETIC CLUB BILBAO (LEZAMA CANTERA)

- **Alevín Año 1º:**

10-year-old players. First year at the Lezama cantera. Everything is new to them at the Club. They are selected among the best players in Bizkaia (Province in The Basque Country), where the Lezama cantera is situated. They play the School Football 7-aside League (clubs also participate) and only in the province of Bizkaia.

- **Alevín 2º año:**

11-year-old players. Second year at the Lezama cantera. They play the School 7-aside League and only in the province of Bizkaia.

- **Infantil 1º año:**

12-year-old players. Third year at the Lezama cantera. They switch to playing 11-aside league football. They play School League amongst the best in Bizkaia.

- **Infantil 2º año:**

Players of 13-year-old and play the School League amongst the best of Bizkaia and some friendly tournaments that have high learning impact. Fourth year at Lezama cantera. A year of pressure because on the pathway to the cadet category they are usually many changes in the players with many of them coming and going.

- **Cadete 1º año:**

14-year-old players and they start playing Federated Football. There are new players coming from other provinces. They play the League in Bizkaia. For some, this is their fifth year at the Lezama cantera.

- **Cadete 2º año:**

Players of 15 years old and play the league in Euskadi (The Basque Country), against more important and stronger clubs. Spain's national team begins at this category.

- **Juvenil 1º año:**

Players aged 16 years old and play the league in the Euskadi (The Basque Country), against teams usually with players' aged one or two years older (high learning demands for the players in this category).

- **Juvenil 2º año:**

Players of 17 years old and play the league in the North zone of Spain, against teams with players generally one year older. They can play in the Spanish Championship and the Spanish Cup.

- **Juvenil 3º año – Basconia (Third Team):**

Players of 18 years old (in youth age). They combine with 19-year-old players on the team. They play the Third Division - Euskadi Group (fourth category of Spain senior). They play against clubs with senior players (very big change and challenge for these players).

- **Bilbao Athletic (2º equipo/ Second Team):**

They play in the Second B or Spanish Second Division. Against senior professional teams.

Lightning Source UK Ltd.
Milton Keynes UK
UKHW021118040522
402471UK00006B/813